Puzzlements
& Predicaments
of the Bible

Puzzlements
& Predicaments
of the Bible

The Weird, the Wacky, and the Wondrous

Linda Washington
Betsy Todt Schmitt
Gene Smillie

HOWARD BOOKS
A DIVISION OF SIMON & SCHUSTER
New York   London   Toronto   Sydney

Our purpose at Howard Books is to:
- *Increase faith* in the hearts of growing Christians
- *Inspire holiness* in the lives of believers
- *Instill hope* in the hearts of struggling people everywhere
Because He's coming again!

Published by Howard Books, a division of Simon & Schuster, Inc.
1230 Avenue of the Americas, New York, NY 10020
www.howardpublishing.com

Puzzlements & Predicaments of the Bible © 2007 The Livingstone Corporation

Library of Congress Cataloging-in-Publication Data

Puzzlements & predicaments of the Bible : the weird, the wacky, and the wondrous / Linda Washington, Betsy Todt Schmitt, Gene Smillie.

p. cm.

ISBN-13: 978-1-4165-6676-2

1. Bible—Miscellanea. I. Schmitt, Betsy. II. Smillie, Gene. III. Title.
IV. Title: Puzzlements and predicaments of the Bible.
BS615.W37 2008
220.6—dc22   2008006545

1 3 5 7 9 10 8 6 4 2

Manufactured in the United States of America

For information regarding special discounts for bulk purchases,
please contact Simon & Schuster Special Sales at 1-800-456-6798
or business@simonandschuster.com.

Interior design by Davina Mock-Maniscalco

Produced with the assistance of The Livingstone Corporation (www.LivingstoneCorp.com). Project staff includes Linda Taylor, Betsy Schmitt, Linda Washington, Gene Smillie, Drenda Thomas Richards, Carol Chaffee Fielding, Mary Horner Collins, Dawn Jett, Will Reaves, Emily Files.

Contents

Introduction

To some people, the Bible is just too weird. They don't read it because they're afraid they won't understand the many puzzlements and predicaments presented in its pages. The Bible *is* a puzzling book. It records some pretty weird events, no doubt about it. *Puzzlements & Predicaments of the Bible* is here to help.

Some of the puzzles are created by cultural issues or by people making odd choices or simply by the way God decides to work in certain situations. One good thing about the Bible: it can withstand any kind of scrutiny. That's why *Puzzlements & Predicaments of the Bible* can jump headlong into the weird, wacky, and wondrous world of the Bible.

- Come along on some "Dangerous Detours," and find out what happens as people follow their own path instead of God's will—like Adam and Eve, Saul, and even Jonah.
- Sit back and shake your head over some of the "Baffling Behaviors" performed by the likes of Noah, Esau, Ruth, Jeremiah, and Nebuchadnezzar—common people and kings do the strangest things.
- Wring your hands over "Sinister Schemes" put in place by such scary people as Delilah, Haman, and Judas.
- Cheer for the "Exceptional Escapes" made by such God-fearing people as Noah, Moses, David,

and Daniel—and even the baby Jesus himself!
- Wonder about why some "Curious Crimes" were considered criminal—like offering the wrong kind of fire or picking wheat on the Sabbath.
- Watch in amazement the "Momentous Miracles" performed by God through Moses, Joshua, Elijah, Elisha, and, of course, Jesus.

Scripture references are provided at the end of each story so you can read the story for yourself. And we encourage you to do so. The Bible might be puzzling, but it needn't be fear inducing. Paul wrote, "All Scripture is given by inspiration of God, and is profitable for doctrine, for reproof, for correction, for instruction in righteousness" (2 Timothy 3:16 NKJV), so even these weird and wacky stories are profitable and can teach us.

So don't be afraid! Dive right in to the puzzlements and predicaments of the Bible!

PART ONE

Dangerous Detours

A Major Mistake

Adam and Eve Detour from God's Explicit Instructions

D O YOU REMEMBER riding in your parents' car on a trip when they got lost, really lost, and didn't know where they were? It's a bad feeling to trust people and then realize they don't know where they are or how to get where they need to go. That's kind of what happened to our original parents, Adam and Eve. They took a pretty big detour, and without God's merciful intervention, humankind would have been forever lost.

It started out as a normal day but one that would end in catastrophe. Eve was caring for the garden when she became intrigued by a beautiful serpent that presented theological twists and turns in a type of conversation she had never experienced before.

The serpent began by asking, "Did God really say, 'You must not eat from any tree in the garden?'" (Genesis 3:1 NIV). It was a gross exaggeration, of course, but a crafty one. It subtly introduced a note of doubt: could God possibly be such a crank, such a mean and greedy person, not to want to share his bounty? "You can't eat from *any* tree?"

"Of course that's not what God said," the lady giggled. How silly! She knew that God had given them everything they needed to eat and drink in that beautiful garden. She and Adam could eat from any tree they liked. Well, . . . all but one. "God did say, 'You must not eat fruit from the tree that is in the middle of the garden, and you must not touch it, or you will die'" (Genesis 3:3).

Oddly enough, God had never told Adam that he couldn't *touch* the tree, just that he couldn't eat from it (see Genesis 2:17). Eve had gotten the "you will die" part right, but the serpent brushed off the idea like cake crumbs from a sleeve. "You won't die," he asserted confidently. "God just doesn't want you to have the same discerning powers that he has—which you will, if you eat from that tree. He's just trying to keep it all for himself. If you eat from that tree, you will be wise like he is."

The woman had never really thought about it before—one tree. Why that one tree? And why put it there if they weren't supposed to eat from it? She looked at the tree more closely. The fruit looked delicious. What was God trying to do anyway? Why would he refuse them something so wonderful? And if eating the fruit from that tree led to knowledge . . . wouldn't that be a good thing?

She reached out her hand and plucked a piece of fruit from the tree.

The serpent grinned.

And humankind started down a detour from which only God could save them.

To read more about this detour of our original parents, see Genesis 3:1–7.

A Forty-Year Detour

God's People Take a Forty-Year Walk to Remember

A RE WE THERE YET?"
Some journeys beg for an ending. The Israelites' journey from Egypt to Canaan was that kind of journey. Footsore and tired of the nomadic life, Israel had earned a rest in the land God promised to give them. So here they were on the last leg of the journey—poised to enter. All that was left to do was spy out the land.

At God's command, Moses chose twelve spies—one from each tribe—to look over the land and bring back some of its fruit. Above all, they were to examine the cities and the people who lived in them.

Off they went to explore, returning after forty days with a humongous cluster of grapes as well as some figs and pomegranates. Fruit was the sign of a lush land. After the spies' report, all the people moved into the land and lived happily ever after . . . except the story doesn't really end that way.

Instead, after talking about the wonderful characteristics of the land, ten of the spies gave a fear-factor assessment of the land's inhabitants and declared, "We are not able to go up against the people, for they are stronger than we are" (Numbers 13:31 ESV). Those people were giants! How could puny Israel hope to defeat people who made them feel like grasshoppers?

Two of the spies—Joshua and Caleb—disagreed with that assessment, knowing that the God of Israel could make even giants seem like grasshoppers. But the people refused to listen to the positive comments of two in the face of the negative comments of ten. Instead, they had a few comments of their own for Moses and Aaron, who often were the brunt of their complaints.

"Why did we leave Egypt?" they whined. "We should go back there." To add insult to injury, they thought about stoning Joshua and Caleb.

God had heard enough. As with the golden calf (see "Mad Cow Disease," p. 39), the people of Israel provoked God to possibly destroy them. But Moses pleaded their case, saying that it would make their enemies think that God was too weak to bring his people into the land.

Once again, God offered forgiveness . . . and consequences. Of all the adults, only Joshua and Caleb would enter the Promised Land. In the meantime, everybody else would wander in the desert for forty years.

Well, the people of Israel couldn't accept no for an answer and decided to try to enter the land anyway. But they were beaten by the Amalekites and other Canaanites and had to retreat in defeat. Perhaps they should have looked to their giant problem-solving God instead of at the giants.

To read more about the Israelites' wanderings, read Numbers 13–14.

THE STARTS AND STOPS OF THE EXODUS

Life as nomads after the exodus was often punctuated by grumblings and groanings from the people of Israel. But along the way, they learned vital lessons from God. Below are some of their journey segments and stopping points. For a fuller list, see Numbers 33:3–49.

WHERE THEY TRAVELED	WHY THEY STOPPED
From Rameses to Succoth and from Succoth to the Red Sea	The people complained, believing themselves trapped at the Red Sea. God parted the Red Sea (Exodus 14:1–15:21).

Where They Traveled	Why They Stopped
From the Red Sea to Marah	The people complained about the bitter water at Marah. When the problem was solved, they traveled to Elim (Exodus 15:22–27).
From Elim to the Desert of Sin	The people complained about the lack of food. God provided manna and quail (Exodus 16).
From the Desert of Sin to Rephidim	The people complained about being thirsty. God provided water out of a rock (Exodus 17:1–7).
From Rephidim to Mount Sinai	God gave Moses the Ten Commandments. While Moses was away, the people sinned by making a golden calf (Exodus 19; 32).
From Mount Sinai to the Desert of Paran	The people finally left Sinai, with Moses' brother-in-law Hobab, who helped advise them about campsites in the desert (Numbers 10:11–36).
From Paran to Taberah	When the people complained in general, fire from the Lord killed some of them (Numbers 11:1–3).
From Taberah to Kibroth Hattaavah	The people complained about the lack of variety in food. God called seventy men to help lead the people. He then sent quail to provide meat for the people. But they felt his wrath when he sent a plague among them (Numbers 11:4–34).
From Kibroth Hattaavah to Hazeroth	Out of jealousy, Miriam and Aaron talked against Moses. God punished Miriam with leprosy (Numbers 11:35–12:15).

WHERE THEY TRAVELED	WHY THEY STOPPED
From Hazeroth to the Desert of Paran	Here the people stopped in order for Moses to send out twelve spies to explore Canaan. The people rebelled when they heard the negative report of ten of the spies. God told them that only their children and Joshua and Caleb would enter the Promised Land. Later, Korah, Dathan, and Abiram rebelled and were killed (Numbers 12:16–19:22).
From the Desert of Zin to Kadesh	Miriam died and was buried at Kadesh. The people grumbled again about their thirst. Out of anger, Moses struck the rock instead of speaking to it and was told he would not enter the Promised Land (Numbers 20:1–13).
From Kadesh to Mount Hor	After the people of Edom refused to allow them to pass through their land, they traveled to Mount Hor, where Aaron died (Numbers 20:14–29).
From Mount Hor to Moab	Along the way to Moab, the king of Arad sent an army against Israel and was defeated. The area was renamed Hormah (Numbers 21:1–3). But as they traveled, the people grumbled against God. He allowed poisonous snakes to bite them. But when a bronze snake was placed on a pole, anyone who looked at it lived (Numbers 21:4–9).
Through Moab	The Israelites camped in a number of places in Moab. God provided water at Beer (Numbers 21:10–20). They fought and defeated Sihon, the Amorite king who did not want them to pass through the land of the Amorites. They later defeated Og, king of Bashan, and took over the land of the Amorites (Numbers 21:21–35).

Where They Traveled	Why They Stopped
Through Moab to the Jordan (across from Jericho)	Balak wanted Balaam to curse the people of Israel. But God refused to allow Balaam to do so (Numbers 22–24). Later, Moses ordered the deaths of those engaged in idolatry and immorality with Moabite women. A plague raged through the camp until Phineas killed two people who engaged in sin (Numbers 25). Later, Israel went to war against Midian (Numbers 31).

A Bad Headache

Sisera Takes a Dangerous Detour into Jael's Tent

THE TIME OF THE JUDGES was a time of peaks and valleys for Israel. Whenever Israel would do "what was evil in the sight of the LORD" (Judges 2:11 ESV), God would allow them to be harassed by enemy nations. Then God would have pity on his people and allow a judge—a deliverer—to lead them against their enemies.

Jabin, a Canaanite king, harassed Israel for twenty years. His hired "muscle" was Sisera—the commander of his army and a formidable foe. His nine hundred chariots were quite a fearsome sight. But in Israel's camp, the handpicked judge was not a man with a bunch of chariots at his disposal, but a woman: Deborah, who also was a prophet.

Deborah had a word from the Lord for Barak, a man chosen to lead Israel's army. He was to assemble ten thousand warriors from two tribes. God would lure Sisera into a trap and give Barak the victory over the enemy.

Despite that promise of victory, Barak vowed that he wouldn't go to war unless Deborah went with him. So Deborah told him, "I will surely go with you. Nevertheless, the road on which you are going will not lead to your glory, for the LORD will sell Sisera into the hand of a woman" (Judges 4:9).

Barak assembled the army as the Lord commanded. And as Deborah prophesied, the battle went overwhelmingly in favor of the Israelites. Sisera made a run for the border, but not in search of Taco Bell. He headed for a tent he could hide in. After a frantic search, the tent of an ally loomed near. This was the tent of Jael.

Jael's husband, Heber, was an ally of Jabin. Jael invited Sisera in and even gave him a drink of milk to quench his thirst.

What more could a man on the run ask for?

Then while Sisera slept, Jael performed a decidedly non-ally action: she grabbed a tent stake and drove it through Sisera's head, killing him instantly.

When Barak came looking for Sisera, Jael showed Barak where Sisera was. Deborah's prophecy had come to pass. Victory was literally at the hands of a woman. Even Barak couldn't help singing about it.

To read more about Sisera, Barak, Deborah, and Jael, see Judges 4–5.

Detour to
the Dark Side

Saul Consults a Witch to Call Up the Spirit of Samuel

MANY PEOPLE enjoy the chills they experience from ghost stories. You can probably name a few classic ghost stories, including "The Legend of Sleepy Hollow" by Washington Irving or the movie *Ghostbusters*. But perhaps the last place you might expect to find a ghost story is in the Bible.

Saul was the first king of Israel. Although God had already anointed his successor (see 1 Samuel 16), Saul was still the king and was facing a battle with the Philistines—the long-term enemies of the Israelites. He wanted some advice as to how to proceed against this strong enemy. But Samuel, the prophet and adviser to the king, had died. And the Lord did not answer Saul's inquiries.

With no adviser on the horizon, Saul decided to consult a medium—someone who claimed to speak to the dead—to find some answers. But Saul's turn to the wild side didn't start there. It began much earlier, when he disobeyed direct orders from God (see 1 Samuel 13–15). He was about to continue that behavior.

One of Israel's laws spoke against mediums: "Do not turn to mediums or consult spiritists, or you will be defiled by them; I am the LORD your God" (Leviticus 19:31 HCSB). Knowing the law, Saul had previously exiled or executed those who claimed to speak to the dead or practiced witchcraft. But in terror and dread of his enemies, he ignored the law this time and went to find the medium who lived in Endor. There, he asked her to call up the ghost of Samuel.

Now the woman was savvy enough to know that his request could be a trap that would lead to her doom. But after Saul assured her that she had nothing to fear, she called up the spirit of Samuel. At that moment she realized the identity of the man before her—King Saul.

Was this really the ghost of Samuel? Whether or not it was, God used this incident to send a message to Saul: Israel would lose the battle against the Philistines. Worse yet, because of Saul's past sins, the kingship would pass to David.

Saul's detour to the dark side led to disaster. First Samuel 31 details Saul's sad end. It just goes to show you that some true ghost stories are really more frightening than those you find in fiction.

This ghost story is recorded in 1 Samuel 28:1–20.

SUICIDES IN THE BIBLE

WHO	WHAT HAPPENED	REFERENCE
Abimelech	Called a suicide since he, as the leader of the army, ordered his armor-bearer to kill him with the sword (having a crushed skull, he apparently did not have the strength to do it himself). He preferred to die at the hands of his male armor-bearer than by the head wound he had received from a woman who dropped a millstone from high above in the tower of Thebez.	Judges 9:50–55

Who	What Happened	Reference
Samson	After his capture by the Philistines at the hands of his girlfriend, Delilah, Samson was put in prison. Some time later, he was taken in chains as the entertainment at a festival in the temple of their god Dagon. The temple was packed with worshipers. They stood Samson between the two great pillars that held up the temple. Since his hair had grown back, Samson used the renewed strength to literally "bring down the house"—on him and everyone else.	Judges 16
Saul	As the Philistine army closed in on Saul and his army, Saul's three sons were killed on Mount Gilboa. Shot by the archers, Saul was severely wounded and begged his armor-bearer to kill him before he could be captured by the enemy. The armor-bearer wouldn't do it, so Saul fell on his own sword.	1 Samuel 31:1–4
Saul's armor-bearer	After King Saul fell on his own sword and killed himself, the armor-bearer did the same.	1 Samuel 31:5
Ahithophel	One of King David's advisers who joined David's son Absalom in rebellion against the king. Later disgraced when his advice was not followed by Absalom, he went home and hanged himself.	2 Samuel 17:1–23

Who	What Happened	Reference
Zimri	King of the northern kingdom of Israel for all of seven days. Zimri had assassinated the previous king (Elah), but the army instead chose Omri as their leader, and they came back from fighting the Philistines to remove Zimri from the throne. When Zimri saw that Tirzah was taken, he went into the citadel of the palace and burned it to the ground over himself.	1 Kings 16:9–20
Judas	When Jesus' disciple Judas realized what was going to happen as a result of his betrayal, he tried to return the money to the religious leaders. But the wheels had been set in motion and nothing would stop them. Judas went out and hanged himself.	Matthew 27:3–5; Acts 1:16–19

A Senseless Census

David's Desire to Count the Fighting Men Angers God

USUALLY, taking a census is not cause for alarm, but in David's case it was.

While David was a godly man and a great king, there were moments in his life that were less than shining. This was one of those moments. It all began when David decided to take a census of the males of fighting age in Israel and Judah.

His chief adviser and commander of the army, Joab, questioned such a step. Why would David need to do such a thing? Here's why: "Satan stood up against Israel and moved David to number Israel" (1 Chronicles 21:1 NASB). David could not be dissuaded from taking the census.

Joab and his men set out on the task of enrolling the fighting men, taking quite a while to accomplish it. "So when they had gone about through the whole land, they came to Jerusalem at the end of nine months and twenty days. And Joab gave the number of the registration of the people to the king; and there were in Israel eight hundred thousand valiant men who drew the sword, and the men of Judah were five hundred thousand men" (2 Samuel 24:8–9 NASB). What a staggering number. This would be quite an impressive army if all were conscripted.

At that point David realized he had sinned by having the men counted. That was one of David's strengths—he could readily admit wrong. As was usually the case when a king sinned, God sent a prophet to talk the matter over with the king. Gad was God's spokesman, who provided David with a chilling choice of punishments:

1. three years of famine,
2. three months of running from an enemy, or
3. three days of plague.

What a choice! Since David didn't seem to favor options 1 and 2, God went with option 3. While three days of plague might not have sounded so bad, David knew what God could do in three days.

When the dust settled after three days of plague, seventy thousand people were dead. But in his compassion, God stopped the angel from destroying more lives when he came to the threshing floor of Araunah the Jebusite.

God sent Gad to David once again with a command: "Go up and build an altar to the LORD on the threshing floor of Araunah the Jebusite" (2 Samuel 24:18 NIV). So David went as God commanded. Araunah offered to give the king his threshing floor, but David refused to take the gift, saying, "I will surely buy it from you for a price, for I will not offer burnt offerings to the LORD my God which cost me nothing" (2 Samuel 24:24 NASB).

When the altar was built and David's sacrifices were offered, God stopped the plague. As usual, David's humility counted with God.

To read more about the census, read 2 Samuel 24 and 1 Chronicles 21.

Jonah Jumps Ship

Jonah Tries to Detour from God and Finds a Fish Instead

"M AN OVERBOARD!" The usual warning cry alerting the crew was not yelled out in Jonah's case. The prophet-turned-fugitive bobbed in the water for a good reason—the crew had thrown him in.

But Jonah jumped ship, metaphorically speaking, even before that. He received the call from the Lord to preach a word of destruction to the city of Nineveh. The Assyrians of this formidable capital city were enemies of the Israelites and were known for their cruelty. The thought of preaching to Nineveh proved so daunting to Jonah that he decided to take a fast ship in the opposite direction— toward Tarshish.

During the trip, a sudden squall battered the ship to the point where it was about to sink. This storm was no coincidence. It was God's way of getting the attention of his disobedient prophet.

While the sailors on the ship panicked, Jonah slept—a feat which amazed the crew. Why wasn't Jonah doing something constructive, such as inquiring of his God the same as everyone else, instead of sleeping?

Per human nature, the crew looked for someone to blame for the fix they were in. They cast lots to determine on whom the blame rested. Lots were dicelike objects used to determine a particular choice. In this case, the lots determined that Jonah was to blame.

Jonah knew the storm was his fault. So at his suggestion, he was hurled into the sea. And what do you know? The storm ceased. But

Jonah didn't flounder in the sea for long. A big fish came and swallowed him whole . . . out of the frying pan and into the fire, so to speak.

Jonah remained in the fish three days and three nights. (Centuries later, Jesus would use this story as a sign that he would remain in the grave three days. See Matthew 12:40.) Jonah had some time on his hands. And he used the time to pray and make things right with God. After he repented, God gave his wayward prophet a second chance.

When the fish deposited Jonah on dry land, God repeated his marching orders: "Go to Nineveh." Jonah wasted no time. He went through the city crying destruction, "Yet forty days and Nineveh will be overthrown" (Jonah 3:4 NASB).

To his amazement, the people chose to repent! They fasted and did the whole nine yards of grieving over their sin. So God decided *not* to destroy the city.

The fourth chapter of Jonah provides Jonah's angry reaction to God's mercy. But God is always the God of second chances. Just ask Jonah.

For more about Jonah's fish adventure, read Jonah 1–3.

Dead Wrong

Ananias and Sapphira Detour from the Truth

MANY PEOPLE have told lies that resulted in the death of a
friendship, a reputation, or an ideal. But most folks don't die
on the spot after telling a lie. Yet Ananias and Sapphira did.

After the arrival of the Holy Spirit on the scene at Pentecost
(see Acts 2), the early church in Jerusalem began to grow. Many believers banded together and shared everything they had. This was
love in action—a marked contrast to the persecution the believers
would soon face. Sometimes, they would sell property and offer the
money to the apostles for the use of the church. Barnabas, a Levite
convert, sold a field and donated the money.

Inspired by the generosity of Barnabas and other believers,
Ananias and his wife, Sapphira, decided to sell their property. In addition, they concocted a plan to keep some of the money and give
the rest to the apostles. Not giving all the money would have been
fine. No one said they had to give *all* the money. But they wanted to
appear to be more generous than they really were. It was a pride
thing. So off went Ananias with his money sack to find Peter.

Peter wasn't fooled by the offering, discerning the culprit at the
root of this false show of generosity: Satan. As he told Ananias,

> Why has Satan filled your heart to lie to the Holy Spirit
> and to keep back for yourself part of the proceeds of the
> land? While it remained unsold, did it not remain your
> own? And after it was sold, was it not at your disposal?

Why is it that you have contrived this deed in your heart?
You have not lied to men but to God. (Acts 5:3–4 ESV)

While Ananias was perfectly within his rights to keep part of the money, the fact that he and his wife lied about the amount was a sin the Holy Spirit did not tolerate. So Ananias died on the spot.

Sapphira soon arrived. When Peter asked her whether or not the money given was the full price of the land, Sapphira agreed with her husband, little knowing that he was dead. Peter gave this stern pronouncement: "How is it that you have agreed together to test the Spirit of the Lord? Behold, the feet of those who have buried your husband are at the door, and they will carry you out" (Acts 5:9). Instantly, Sapphira died too!

Two deaths like that made an impression on the members of the church. They were absolutely terrified. But they learned one important thing: Lying to the Holy Spirit could be fatal.

To read more about this story, read Acts 4:36—5:11.

STRANGE DEATHS IN THE BIBLE

WHO	STRANGE DEATH	REFERENCE
People of Sodom and Gomorrah	Fire and burning sulfur raining down from heaven	Genesis 19:24–25
Lot's Wife	Turned into a pillar of salt	Genesis 19:26
Nadab and Abihu	Burned by fire at the altar	Leviticus 10:1–2
Korah, Dathan, and Abiram and their families	Swallowed up by the ground	Numbers 16:31–34
Sisera	Had a tent peg driven into his head	Judges 4:21
Abimelech	Had a millstone thrown from a tower above him that split his skull	Judges 9:52–53

WHO	STRANGE DEATH	REFERENCE
Unnamed concubine	Raped to death	Judges 19
Eli	Broke his neck falling out of a chair	1 Samuel 4:18
Uzzah	Struck dead for touching the ark of the covenant	2 Samuel 6:6–7
Absalom	Caught by his hair in a tree; stabbed in the heart while hanging there helpless	2 Samuel 18:9–15
Ahaziah's guards	Consumed by fire from heaven	2 Kings 1:9–12
Youths of Bethel	Mauled by bears	2 Kings 2:23–25
Jezebel	Thrown out of a window	2 Kings 9:33
Job's Children	House collapsed in a windstorm	Job 1:18–19
Nebuchadnezzar's soldiers	Killed by the heat of the fire as they threw Shadrach, Meschach, and Abednego into the furnace	Daniel 3:22
Darius's officials	Bones crushed by lions	Daniel 6:24
Ananias and Sapphira	Struck dead by God—separately—because of their lies	Acts 5:1–11
Herod Agrippa I	Eaten by worms	Acts 12:20–23

Cat Fight

Euodia and Syntyche Take a Detour from Unity

WHAT IF one brief moment in your life, one lapse of judgment, one stupid incident, were caught in freeze-frame and you were forever remembered for that one thing? That's what happened to Euodia and Syntyche, two women active in the church in Philippi. As Paul brought his letter to the Philippians to a close, he added these words of reprimand:

> Now I appeal to Euodia and Syntyche. Please, because you belong to the Lord, settle your disagreement. And I ask you, my true partner, to help these two women, for they worked hard with me in telling others the Good News. They worked along with Clement and the rest of my co-workers, whose names are written in the Book of Life. (Philippians 4:2–3 NLT)

These women are known today only because their constant arguing called for special attention from the apostle Paul.

How embarrassing.

When people get to heaven, do they look up Euodia and Syntyche to find out what their catfight was all about? "Yeah, I read about you in the Bible—book of Philippians. So what was that all about anyway?" The two women probably roll their eyes, look at each other, and really, really wish they'd settled their disagreement sooner.

We know these women were Christians and were part of the church in Philippi. They worked with Paul in evangelizing and worked "hard," he wrote. They worked with Clement and other co-workers to help spread the good news. They were busy women whose work apparently had effective results.

So what in the world went wrong?

We'll never know (unless they're answering the question in heaven). Whatever their disagreement, it was causing concern and friction in the rest of the church body. In other words, the disagreement had further-reaching consequences than just being a catfight over the color of the tablecloths at the church picnic. It's possible that these women held some kind of leadership posts or at least positions of responsibility. What they disagreed about may have been important—but apparently not important enough for Paul to mention any doctrinal problem. However, their fight was getting in the way of their mission, and it may well have been having a negative effect on those whom they had led to faith. So Paul wanted them to stop fighting. He pleaded with them to do whatever it would take to settle their disagreement; he even asked another church member to moderate if necessary. Euodia and Syntyche needed to get back to the important task of spreading the good news.

It doesn't take much for us to get angry with someone else, does it? While we can't expect to be best friends with every person in our little world, we should at least heed Paul's advice, "Do all that you can to live in peace with everyone" (Romans 12:18 NLT). We shouldn't be arguing with our brothers and sisters in Christ or whining about not getting our own way. Instead, we need to be going about the work of the kingdom. That would make Paul proud.

Euodia and Syntyche are mentioned in Philippians 4:2–3.

PART TWO:

Baffling Behaviors

Indecent Exposure

Noah Gets Drunk—a Sad Aftermath to a Powerful Adventure

WE LIKE OUR HEROES large and in charge, don't we? There's nothing quite like watching cinema-hero Indiana Jones swing on his whip or wall-crawling Spider-Man cleverly battle the bad guys. But we don't like to see our heroes falter, even on screen. That creates tension within us. We forget that heroes are still human beings with problems.

This is especially true with Bible characters we admire. Take Noah. He "was a righteous man, blameless among the people of his time, and he walked with God" (Genesis 6:9 NIV). The rest of the world was going to the dogs, but "Noah found favor in the eyes of the LORD" (Genesis 6:8). Out of the entire human race, Noah was chosen for God's great plan. He survived the ridicule of his friends and neighbors and built an ark before the great Flood (see "Flood Insurance," p. 119). As far as heroes go, Noah was larger than life. But then picture this: Noah sprawled in a tent, dead drunk. This snapshot almost needs a "What's wrong with this picture?" caption.

There's something about Noah's ark-story epilogue that makes us uncomfortable. As the story unfolds in Genesis 9:18–27, we see Noah and his family trying to rebuild their lives after the Flood. (Hear the hopeful music playing in the background?) We have a sense of life continuing, until we get to the part of the story where Noah plants a vineyard. (Cue the ominous music.) Noah proceeds to enjoy the fruit of the vine to an excessive degree.

Noah's being passed out in his tent, completely exposed in more

ways than one, displays a depth of sad vulnerability we aren't prepared for. And neither was his son Ham, who found his father in
this condition. Ham quickly spread the word to his brothers—Shem
and Japheth. But Shem and Japheth reacted in a way to preserve
their father's dignity. Instead of boldly walking in to gawk, they
walked into the tent *backward* to avoid seeing him. They carried
with them a garment to drop over their father to cover his nudity.

Noah was all too human—just like the rest of us. He had his
good days and his bad days. God undoubtedly knew Noah's foibles
when he assigned the ark-building task to him in the first place.

Some stories don't have the rosiest of endings. Sometimes
human nature gets in the way and makes everything a mess. But
God ultimately has the last word. He can use us for his service,
sometimes in spite of our foibles!

This incident with Noah and his sons is recorded in Genesis 9:18–27.

Lot's Family Values

Lot Raises His Family in the Evil City of Sodom

GOOD REALTORS say that the most important consideration
in buying a house is "location, location, location." Many
parents base their decisions about where to plant their families on
good neighborhoods and good schools. They want a good and safe
environment for their children. So we might scratch our heads at

Lot's choosing the city of Sodom as a place to settle and raise his kids. Sodom's reputation was a bit blackened (pun intended).

But let's back up . . . who was Lot? He was Abram's nephew. Abram (later called Abraham) was the friend of God and the father of Isaac. (But that's another story.) Uncle Abram was a man of incredible wealth with a huge entourage. Lot also had a huge household and tons of livestock. What happens when two people with large households and lots of livestock live in the same area? They clash. You can almost hear both sides saying, "This town ain't big enough for the both of us."

In this case, the entire plain of Jordan stretched out before them, so there was room to spread out. Abram, being an honorable man, offered Lot the first pick. "The whole countryside is open to you. Take your choice of any section of the land you want, and we will separate. If you want the land to the left, then I'll take the land on the right. If you prefer the land on the right, then I'll go to the left" (Genesis 13:9 NLT). With "location, location, location" in mind, Lot chose the best place—the land that was "well watered everywhere" (Genesis 13:10). Water was an extremely important consideration in an arid land, and the Eden-like setting seemed ideal to Lot. But there was a problem in paradise: "The people of this area were extremely wicked and constantly sinned against the LORD" (Genesis 13:13).

Imagine building a dream house next door to a crack house or an adult bookstore. This was basically Lot's choice when he moved his household close to Sodom. This was not a place known for its family values. Perhaps Lot felt that he was entitled to the "best" land. Sometimes the "best" choice turns out to be the worst. Genesis 19 recounts the sad aftermath of Lot's choice of location. He should have looked more closely at his neighborhood before making that decision.

Read about Lot's choice in Genesis 13:10–13.

Sacrifice *What?*

Abraham Goes to Moriah to Sacrifice Isaac

THE JOURNEY must have seemed awfully strange to the young man Isaac. He and his father slowly climbed the steep hill to offer a sacrifice, but they hadn't brought any animal to slaughter on the makeshift stone altar. Isaac carried a heavy bundle of firewood, knowing there'd be precious little combustible fuel above timber line. He breathed heavily, pausing for a moment to look back down the slope. In the distance he could make out the forms of the two servants his father had instructed to stay behind and wait for their return.

The servants had provided an atmosphere of adventure and fun the first few days of the trip to this sacred mountain. But now they were mere specks on the landscape, and Isaac was limited to the company of his taciturn elderly father, Abraham, who hadn't said a word since they began climbing. His father seemed to be deep in thought. Isaac finally dared to break the silence. He asked about something that puzzled him, flying around in his mind like a pesky horsefly.

"Father?"

"Yes, my son?"

"Father, we have the wood for the burnt offering, we have the fire, we have the knife to kill the animal for the offering . . . but where is the lamb for the sacrifice?"

Did Abraham pause for a split second? Did he choke back tears? Or did he just naturally reply, as it appears in the text? He said, "God himself will provide the lamb for the burnt offering, my son" (Genesis 22:8 NIV). All we know is what we read. Then it follows with, "And the two of them went on together."

Silence returned. What *could* that old man have been thinking as he made his way laboriously up that hill? He had waited for Isaac, this promised son, for twenty-five long years, ever since the Lord first made a covenant with him. Then, against all possible natural expectation, a baby boy was indeed born in Abraham's hundredth year, to a wrinkled wife only ten years younger than himself! They both laughed themselves silly with the exuberant hilarity of it all, and all their neighbors loved the joke as well.

He cherished this boy walking beside him more than anything or anyone. His love for Isaac knew no bounds. Not only was Isaac's birth itself miraculous, but God had given Abraham glimpses of the glory that would accrue to all "his descendants." This boy would be the ancestor of kings and kingdoms, of a progeny greater in number than the starry host that formed the celestial canopy over their heads at night.

And now Abraham trudged up the mount of Moriah to obey God's command: "Take your son, your only son, Isaac, whom you love, and go to the region of Moriah. Sacrifice him there as a burnt offering on one of the mountains I will tell you about" (Genesis 22:2). It was too impossible, too bizarre. There could be no understanding, no bargaining. This was a test of pure obedience, and pure obedience was the only right response.

Once at the place, father and son set to work building an altar from the stones lying around. Methodically, almost mechanically, Abraham stacked the wood on the altar, tied up Isaac, and carefully stretched him out on top of the wood. Then he leaned over, picked up the knife, and raised it over his head to bring it crashing down on his beloved son.

"Abraham!" called out the angel of the Lord. "Put down the knife, and untie the boy. You have not withheld your most precious possession, your only son, from me. That's what I wanted to see."

And those of us who live four centuries removed from that scene can also see a deeper meaning in it all, for just as the ram was provided to Abraham as a substitute for his son, so centuries later, in this very location, Jesus of Nazareth would be crucified as a substitute for us. So maybe part of what was happening that day was that God let Abraham taste just a little of the bittersweet pain and love that he, the Father, would experience when the day came to offer *his* son in sacrifice.

To read more about Abraham and Isaac, see Genesis 21–22.

FAMOUS MOUNTAINS [AND PEAKS AND HILLS] IN THE BIBLE

MOUNTAIN	REFERENCE	WHAT HAPPENED THERE
Ararat (mountains of)	Genesis 8:4	Noah's ark landed.
Moriah	Genesis 22:2	Abraham was sent there to sacrifice Issac.
Gilead (hill country of)	Genesis 31:20–49	Jacob and Laban came to terms with their past differences.
Sinai (Horeb)	Exodus 3:1–2	Moses was spoken to by the burning bush.
Sinai	Exodus 20–31	Moses received the Ten Commandments and other instructions for the nation of Israel.
Hor	Numbers 20:22–29	Burial place of Aaron
Pisgah Peak	Deuteronomy 3:27	Moses saw the Promised Land from this peak.
Ebal	Deuteronomy 11:29	Curses upon Israel were pronounced from this peak, while across the valley . . .
Gerizim	Deuteronomy 11:29	. . . blessings upon Israel were pronounced from this peak.
Tabor	Judges 4:6–15	Barak defeated Sisera.

MOUNTAIN	REFERENCE	WHAT HAPPENED THERE
Gilboa	1 Samuel 31:1–6	Saul and Jonathan died fighting the Philistines.
Lebanon (mountain range)	1 Kings 5:6–14	Provided the cedar wood for Solomon's temple
Carmel	1 Kings 18:19	Elijah took on the priests of Baal.
Hermon	Matthew 17:1–13; Mark 9:2–13; Luke 9:28–36	Traditionally considered to be the site of Jesus' Transfiguration.
Olives	Matthew 24–25	Where Jesus last taught before entering Jerusalem

Broth for a Birthright

Esau Sells His Future for a Bowl of Stew

I'M SO HUNGRY I could eat a horse!" "I'm starving!" "My kingdom for a hamburger!" Hunger pangs can make us say things we don't really mean or promise things we don't really intend to do. That's the story of Esau. Unfortunately, Esau not only exaggerated his hunger but also acted rashly because of it. And it cost him dearly.

The elder of twin sons born to Isaac and Rebekah, Esau was the polar opposite of his brother, Jacob. Esau was covered with hair from birth; Jacob was smooth skinned. Esau was the outdoorsy type, preferring to spend his time hunting and bringing home the food. Jacob was a homebody, more interested in honing his culinary skills and preparing the meals.

As the firstborn son, Esau was the rightful heir to his family's inheritance. In fact, he was entitled to double the inheritance in addition to the honor of becoming the family's leader. Now Esau could sell his birthright or give it away if he wanted, but in doing so he would lose everything—the family fortune and the leadership role. So having the birthright was very desirable, and it was the one thing that Jacob craved.

On this particular day, Esau returned to the family tent, exhausted and hungry after a long day on the hunt. His brother, who had spent a quiet day at home, was at the fire putting the finishing touches on his stew. Esau took one whiff of the tantalizing aroma and demanded, "I'm starved! Give me some of that red stew you've made."

Never one to miss an opportunity, Jacob replied slyly, "Fine. But trade me your birthright for it," to which Esau unwisely retorted, "Look, I'm dying of starvation. What good is my birthright to me right now?"

In a matter of seconds, the deal was sealed. Jacob, knowing that he had better make the transaction ironclad, asked his brother to swear an oath that the birthright was now his. Esau, positively salivating by now, quickly agreed. So Esau happily walked off with a heaping bowl of lentils and bread while Jacob delighted in the fact that the family birthright was now his.

Food for fortune? Lentils for leadership? What was Esau thinking? Obviously, he was not thinking of his future. His only thought was about instant gratification; satisfying his hunger right there and then. Esau was in no danger of starving, yet he used that thought to justify his actions. After all, so he reasoned, if he actually did starve to death, what good was his inheritance? But it was a short-term solution that, in the long run, cost Esau his future.

Read the story of Esau's choice in Genesis 25:29–34.

A Tempting Offer

Tamar Disguises Herself as a Prostitute for an Unusual Reason

THROUGHOUT THE BIBLE there are stories of barren women who longed to have children. Sarah (see Genesis 16), Rachel (see Genesis 30), Hannah (see 1 Samuel 1), and Elizabeth (see Luke 1), just to name a handful. In those days, children were viewed as a direct blessing from God (see Psalms 37:26; 127:3), and a woman without children probably felt "cursed" and certainly felt shamed. During Bible times, a woman's security and livelihood revolved around hearth and home. If she didn't have a husband and children, what did she have? Not much.

Add Tamar to the above list of childless women. She was the daughter-in-law of Judah (a brother of Joseph and the son of Jacob). There was already enough dysfunction in Judah's family to fuel several episodes of a soap opera (see Genesis 37). This story just adds to the sad saga.

Judah was the proud father of three sons: Er, Onan, and Shelah. When Er grew up, Judah found a wife for him—Tamar. But this was no fairy-tale marriage. Er had the unfortunate reputation of being "so evil" that there was only one solution: "The LORD put him to death" (Genesis 38:7 NIV). That's pretty evil. But what was Tamar to do?

According to the law of Israel, if a man died before his wife could conceive, his brother had to marry the widow and raise up sons in the name of the dead man. This was known as a levirate marriage. A resentful Onan married Tamar, but took measures to prevent her from conceiving. Obviously, he was a contestant in the evil sweepstakes like his older brother. So God put him to death as well (see Genesis 38:8–10).

Seeing the number of his sons steadily dwindle, Judah wanted to hang on to young Shelah. He suggested that Tamar return to her father's home, with the excuse that Shelah needed to become a man first before marrying Tamar.

After waiting and waiting, still-childless Tamar decided to take matters into her own hands. Never underestimate what a desperate woman will do! She disguised herself and waited for her father-in-law, Judah, on the road to Timnah, knowing that he would travel there to shear his sheep. Assuming that Tamar was a temple prostitute, Judah quickly sought her services for the price of a goat. Tamar agreed, but demanded an assurance of his payment: Judah's seal, the cord around it, and his staff. When Judah returned home, the goat was sent, but Tamar could not be found.

Months later Tamar appeared noticeably pregnant. After learning that Tamar was accused of prostitution, Judah reacted with righteous indignation and demanded that she be burned to death. But when Tamar revealed his staff, seal, and cord, Judah realized his fault in the matter and spared her life.

Tamar gave birth to twin sons—Perez and Zerah—and is one of the few women mentioned in the genealogy of Jesus (see Matthew 1:3). This genealogy reveals a long list of desperate people in the ancestry of Jesus, and the gracious God who championed them.

Read this unusually desperate attempt to have children in Genesis 38.

Sticky Stubbornness

Even after All the Plagues, Pharaoh Refuses to Give In

FROM THE FIRST DAY Moses walked into Pharaoh's court—asking Pharaoh to let the Hebrews go—until the day he walked out for the last time, Pharaoh was a hard case. He was the type who might say, "I know that God doesn't exist. Even if God showed himself to me, I wouldn't believe it." Stubborn, even after watching sign after sign after sign of God's power fall on his kingdom, literally "fall" on his kingdom, as cisterns filled up with blood where there had been fresh water before, as millions of frogs hopped about uncontrollably throughout Egyptian households, and as gnats whirled around by the millions.

Pharaoh's own court magicians told him, "You know, this whole thing has the fingerprint of God on it. Maybe you should listen to this guy Moses." But Pharaoh made his heart more stubborn yet.

Soon thick swarms of flies covered the Egyptians' heads and those of their animals, until all one could see throughout Egypt were black masses of flies filling the air everywhere—except where the Israelites lived. There, the plagues had no effect whatsoever, just as God had predicted through Moses.

After the flies, a deadly disease fell on the land, killing all the Egyptians' livestock. The king was not softened, however, by this further evidence of God's sovereignty, so he and his court, and everyone else in Egypt, had to endure yet another plague. Soot from a kiln thrown into the air by Moses caused great painful boils to break out on the skin of everyone in the land. Pharaoh's servants, covered with festering boils, looked at him in awe, in misery, and in disbelief as he stubbornly persisted in refusing to acknowledge God.

"All right, then," intoned Moses, "if you still won't believe, God says he will send hail and lightning, destruction like you've never seen before and no one will ever see again."

And sure enough it was so. The next morning, thunder, hail, and fire came crashing down out of heaven, smashing every green living plant and tree to splinters of broken fiber. And as if that weren't enough, God then sent a sky-darkening cloud of locusts that finished off every last bite of whatever might have been left to eat in Egypt.

Pharaoh's officials looked at him in disgust and horror. "What in the world is the matter with you?" they hissed, not even bothering to pretend to be polite. "Don't you understand that Egypt is ruined? You've rejected God over and over, and each time he sends more devastating evidence that he is in total control of the situation. Can't you see any of this? It is obvious to everyone but you apparently."

And it was obvious to everyone but Pharaoh. He, in contrast, endured two more devastating plagues, due to his sticky stubbornness. Then he was vanquished. He wearily waved Moses and the Israelites out of the land and sat back to count his losses. But like buyer's remorse, he suddenly had a case of "Pharaoh's remorse" and decided to try to recoup his losses. He pursued them to the edge of the Red Sea. Sticky stubbornness indeed!

To discover more about Moses' encounters with Pharaoh, read Exodus 7–14.

Mad Cow Disease

A Golden Calf Spells Trouble for the Israelites

THE EFFECTS of mad cow disease, also known as *bovine spongiform encephalopathy*, are terrible. Since the 1990s, when humans started dying of the virulent disease, new regulations have been put into effect to prevent others from succumbing. But this wasn't the first time a cow caused trouble for humans. (And no, we're not thinking of Mrs. O'Leary's cow that allegedly started the Chicago fire of 1871.) Another kind of cow caused great trouble for the people of Israel. Here's the story.

Having finally escaped from Egypt (see "Sticky Stubbornness," p. 37), the people of Israel traveled through the wilderness to their new home—the Promised Land of Canaan. But in the midst of their travels, they had to make a pit stop at Mount Sinai, where Moses went to pick up a law or two, also known as the Ten Commandments.

Moses stayed up on the mountain for over a month. Having been privy to the crashing and booming of the lightning as God arrived on Mount Sinai to converse with Moses (see Exodus 19), the people weren't so sure that Moses would live through the conversation. So they decided, "Hey, why shouldn't we have gods like the ones in Egypt?"

You might well wonder why they would leap to such a conclusion. Having lived as slaves in Egypt for many generations, the people of Israel often fell away from God during fearful situations.

Moses, who talked directly to God and heard his voice, kept them on the straight and narrow.

The Egyptians worshiped multiple idols, including a bull god. Whether this golden calf was meant to emulate that god can only be speculated. Regardless, the Israelites demanded that Moses' brother, Aaron, make the calf for them. After gathering the gold jewelry of the people, Aaron had the calf made. But even after doing that, he requested that the people hold a festival for the Lord God. So the people held their festival and were satisfied with their golden calf.

Meanwhile up on the mountain, God informed Moses of the problem below and of his plan to destroy the people. God was rather candid about what he planned to do. But even though he was angry, God didn't immediately blast away. He waited to see what Moses would say about the plan.

Moses pleaded on behalf of the people and won a reprieve for them. But when he climbed off the mountain to see for himself what was occurring, he grew angry! The tablets that God carved out of the mountain were soon on a collision course with the foot of the mountain. Smash! The perfect illustration of how the people already broke the laws.

It was time to clean house. After sternly confronting Aaron, Moses gave the people an ultimatum: if you're on the Lord's side, come stand by Moses. Now.

When the Levites ran to stand by Moses, he gave them a grisly command: go through the camp and kill those who sided against the Lord. About three thousand people died. But the pain was not over yet. On the following day, although Moses prayed for the people, the Lord sent an angel to strike them with a disease.

The Bible doesn't tell us what type of plague they suffered or whether anyone died of it. But the sad fact remains that this particular strain of "mad cow disease" had another name—idolatry.

The full story of the golden calf is found in Exodus 32.

Keep Walkin'

A Walk around Jericho Knocks Down the City Walls

REPETITIVE TASKS can make us crazy, especially when we have to do something we think makes us look foolish (the hokey pokey, for example). But imagine being told to walk around a city once a day for six or seven days, being assured that you would own that city if you kept up the task. Would you keep walkin'? You would if you were Joshua and the Israelites.

In order for the Israelites to conquer the Promised Land, God told Joshua to go up against Jericho and God would deliver it into their hands. Now Jericho was a fortified city with a double-thick wall. It looked impregnable. But as impressive as the wall looked, there was one thing in the Israelites' favor: their God had an awesome and frightening reputation! Double walls or not, the people of Jericho were afraid. "Jericho was tightly shut up because of the Israelites. No one went out and no one came in" (Joshua 6:1 NIV). Earlier, the spies had found out through Rahab the prostitute that rumors about the might of the God of Israel had reached the people of Jericho (see Joshua 2:8–13).

Joshua, the leader of the people of Israel after Moses died, was given the battle plan by his Commander-in-Chief. God ordered, "March around the city once with all the armed men. Do this for six days. Have seven priests carry trumpets of rams' horns in front of the ark. On the seventh day, march around the city seven times, with the priests blowing the trumpets" (Joshua 6:3–4).

Riiiiiight. Sure thing, Lord. This was not exactly a plan to inspire confidence. But God didn't want the people to be confident in their prowess or how they looked. He wanted them to be confident in him. So Joshua and the people of Israel followed the plan to the letter. Disobedience was simply not an option.

Imagine living in Jericho that week, watching an army silently march around the city each day, carrying with them a strange box. How would it feel? One might think, *Those rumors I heard about the powerful Israelites can't be true. They look weird.*

Day 1: March.

Day 2: March.

Day 3: March.

You get the picture. They kept walkin'. On the seventh day as per the plan, the people marched around the city seven times. The excitement was growing. After the seventh time around, the priests blew a loud trumpet blast. Joshua gave the people the signal to shout. At that moment, the walls of this impregnable city feel to the ground. The city was theirs! All because the Israelites chose to keep walkin' just the way God told them to. Before burning the city, Joshua commanded the two spies to rescue Rahab and her family. And Rahab chose to keep walkin' with the Israelites too.

Joshua and the Israelites keep walkin' around Jericho in Joshua 6.

Fleeced

Gideon Sets Out a Fleece to Get a Sign from God

THOUGH THE BIBLE shows many varying and diverse examples of divine direction, the one story that is probably the most famous is the one about Gideon and his fleece.

The ironic thing is, though, that this fleece business was not about determining what God wanted Gideon to do. All that had already been announced earlier to Gideon, with authority, by the angel of the Lord. The issue for Gideon, from the first time the angel appeared and each time he spoke with the Lord after that, was whether this really was the Word of God or not. "Is this *really* you?" The Lord's presence, his palpable authority and power to realize what he proposed, was what Gideon wanted to be sure of.

Thus, when the angel first found him hiding from the mighty Midianites, surreptitiously gleaning a few stalks of wheat under cover of a wine press, the angel greeted him with the words, "The LORD is with you, mighty warrior" (Judges 6:12 NIV), an expression that struck Gideon as ludicrous incongruity. He stopped skulking around for a moment and gave a somewhat sarcastic response: "If the LORD is with us, why has all this happened to us? Where are all his wonders that our fathers told us about when they said, 'Did not the LORD bring us up out of Egypt?' But now the LORD has abandoned us and put us into the hand of Midian" (Judges 6:13).

The angel wasn't going to slide a fast one past this young farmer. Gideon knew what to expect from God. He'd heard all the tales of God's supernatural help to their forefathers—help that had been

conspicuously absent of late. "Don't tell me 'the Lord is with you,'"
he countered, "unless you're ready to prove it."

God was not put off by Gideon's challenge to "prove himself."
Repeatedly, when Gideon sought reassurance that this really was
God who was spurring him on to action, God gave him the signs he
asked for, including the famous wool fleece: moist with dew one
night while the ground all around was dry; then the following night
the opposite scenario—ground covered with dew while the fleece
lying in the middle of all that condensation was perfectly dry. Yes,
God would use him to win this battle. Even though the odds were
135,000 to 300, Gideon believed and acted.

We don't need a fleece. If we want guidance, God promises to
give it. And when we've got that reassurance in our back pocket, we
can take on all odds.

To read more about Gideon's fleece, see Judges 6:33–40.

Dog Soldiers

*God Maximizes a Minimum of Troops to Defeat the
Midianites*

EPIC MOVIES such as *The Lord of the Ring: The Return of the
King* and *Braveheart* feature the grand sweeping drama of war
as two armies clash against each other. It's natural to root for the
underdog army, the one vastly outnumbered and fighting on the side

of good. So start rooting for Gideon, because in the battle with the Midianites, Gideon's men were really underdogs.

Gideon's army was certainly on the side of good, being commissioned by God to fight against the combined forces of the Midianites and the Amalekites. Initially Gideon had thirty-two thousand men marching beside him. He may have felt good about that whole safety-in-numbers thing and may have thought, *Hey, we can take on these guys*. During the inspection of the troops, however, God—the real Commander-in-Chief—had a surprising announcement for Gideon: "There are too many men. Just so you won't boast about beating the Midianites in your won strength, ask anyone who is afraid to turn back now."

Too many? Turn back?! Perhaps these were the conflicting thoughts of Gideon as he shared God's message with the men. Imagine his face when he actually saw twenty-two thousand of those troops turn around and leave.

Oh well. At least there were still ten thousand men to take to war. The cushion of comfort was still in place.

But God wasn't finished. "Too many men still. I will weed them out for you." He went on to tell Gideon to take them to the nearest body of water. The determining factor for who would go and who wouldn't go was this: Those who lapped the water the way a dog would drink it were the troops to take into battle. All of the others were to be sent home.

Imagine Gideon as he watched the men drink. Perhaps he thought, *Come on, men! We need big numbers here!* But only three hundred of the ten thousand lapped the water in the right way.

God was satisfied with that number and assured Gideon that he would help them defeat the Midianites. God also had another piece of advice. Gideon was to take his servant Purah and check out the enemy troops. So they did, and this is what they saw: "The Midianites and the Amalekites and all the sons of the east were lying in the valley as numerous as locusts; and their camels were without number, as numerous as the sand on the seashore" (Judges 7:12 NASB).

Heard of the Battle of Thermopylae between the vast Persian army and three hundred Spartan Greeks? (Hint: the Greeks lost after a valiant last stand.) Such were the odds faced by Gideon and his soldiers. But instead of the slaughter faced by the Spartans, God had another ending in mind.

During his tour of the enemy camp, Gideon overheard a Midianite man recounting a dream to his friend. In his dream, the man had seen a barley loaf roll into the Midianite camp and strike the tent of the Midianites. From this, the friend determined that Gideon's troops would be victorious.

Heartened, Gideon ran back to ready his troops. But instead of arming them in the usual way (swords and bows and arrows), he gave them trumpets and empty jars with torches! After they advanced to the perimeter of the Midianite troops, Gideon gave the signal. The men blew the trumpets, broke the jars, and cried, "A sword for the LORD and for Gideon!" (Judges 7:20).

The Midianites and the Amalekites panicked and fled! Then Gideon and his troops gave chase, after which Gideon sent out an all-points bulletin to the other Israelite troops to come and join the hunt.

God used a small ragtag army to defeat the enemy troops and proved that overwhelming victory is always possible with a big God.

Read about this battle in Judges 7.

Sleepless in Bethlehem

Ruth Sleeps at Boaz's Feet

THE BIBLE is full of tales of romances and betrothals, twisted courtships, and arranged matches that turned out amazingly well. It portrays the first stirrings of young love and the patient perseverance of lifelong partnerships. It does not shrink from revealing flings and flirtations, seedy secret gropings, and even the vile reality of rape. But once in a while a biblical writer will pause to focus on a love story simply, it seems, because it is so sweet. Ruth is one of those stories.

Oh, sure, it's an important story to include in the canon, because Ruth ends up being the great-grandmother of King David (and thus an ancestor of the Messiah). It's also important because of the "kinsman redeemer" motif that saturates the story (reminding us of Jesus the Redeemer). Yes, we know all that. But let's be frank: what a great, uplifting, and exciting love story! And the scene in which Ruth, at the advice of her wise old mother-in-law, slips under the covers of aging-but-still-virile Boaz is stirring and provocative, though by no means salacious. We can't avert our eyes and ears from what will follow when Boaz awakes in the dark, feels her warmth at his feet, and realizes what she offers.

The wholesomeness of the customs alluded to in this story are underlined by Naomi's careful instructions to Ruth:

> Wash and perfume yourself, and put on your best clothes.
> Then go down to the threshing floor, but don't let him

know you are there until he has finished eating and drinking. When he lies down, note the place where he is lying. Then go and uncover his feet and lie down. He will tell you what to do. (Ruth 3:3–4 NIV)

Wise old lady! "Get yourself nice and clean, put on some good-smelling ointment, some nice clothes, and then discreetly, without calling attention to yourself, just place yourself humbly at his feet. He'll take it from there." She was right; he did.

The earlier chapters of the book of Ruth already alerted us to the fact that Boaz had noticed Ruth's qualities: her loyalty to her mother-in-law, her humility, her care of the older lady, and her apparent lack of interest in "fooling around" with younger fellows out in the fields, as was wont to happen in harvest time. So when he awoke, he was at first astonished that someone of the female gender had placed herself under his blanket and was asking for his protection; then he was delighted, and apparently honored, to discover that she had chosen him, rather than a younger man, to replace her dead husband. He immediately assented to the responsibilities of taking care of her and her household. He poured out a generous helping of the barley harvest as a gift, showing his good will and intentions, and sent her home before dawn, insisting on discretion about their passing the night together until he could arrange for things to be done in a kosher manner.

And as Naomi assured Ruth upon her return, "Wait, my daughter, until you find out what happens. For the man will not rest until the matter is settled today" (Ruth 3:18). She was right. He didn't wait an hour. He went right to the heart of the local legal system, deftly pushed aside a possible rival for the hand of Ruth, and concluded the binding legalities that made him one with Ruth—man and wife.

Not long after, a son was born to them, who gave joy to everyone involved in the story. And it appears that "they lived happily ever after."

To read more about Ruth and Boaz, read Ruth 3–4.

Duel on Mount Carmel

Elijah Soaks the Sacrifice to Prove That God Is the Real God

HOW DOES ONE PROVE that God is at work? Try this one: Elijah wanted to show the difference between the God of Israel and the "not god" Baal of the Canaanites. So he challenged the priests of Baal to a direct contest in front of the assembled masses of the nation.

"Let's get up on top of a high mountain where nobody can go duckin' and dodgin'," he called out. "We'll see whose god is the real God. Each of us should place a sacrifice on our respective altars. We'll call on the god we believe in to answer with fire, and whoever drops fire down out of heaven on the sacrifice and consumes it, we'll know *that* one is the true God."

The tribes of Israel were immediately enchanted by the simplicity and directness of the challenge and answered, "Yes! That's a great idea. Let's do it."

On that Baal side, most nodded their heads, though some of them looked at each other as if to say, "Uh-oh, can we do this?" Elijah graciously gave the Baalists first shot. "Go ahead, fellas," he said, "you first. Give it everything you've got."

They did, too. They danced and they howled, and when there was no response, they howled some more. They began to cut themselves with knives so they bled profusely, trying to get the attention of their god, who, it seemed, was indifferent or deaf or on a coffee break or something. Elijah made the most of their embarrassment, calling out ironically, "You'll have to shout louder. . . . Perhaps he is daydreaming, or is relieving himself. Or maybe he is away on a trip, or is asleep and needs to be wakened!" (1 Kings 18:27 NLT). They shouted, to no avail, all day. Really. All . . . day. By late afternoon they were exhausted, to say nothing of vitiated and anemic from extreme blood loss, and, to put it bluntly, humiliated. There had been no answer from Baal.

Then Elijah quietly said, "Okay it's my turn. Israel, gather around me here." The people drew close to watch Elijah. He reconstructed a torn-down altar of twelve stones, one for each tribe of Israel. He piled wood on it, then cut up a bull and arranged it on top of the wood . . . and then Elijah did the strangest thing that anyone had ever seen in conjunction with burned sacrifices. He called for four barrels of water to be brought up and poured over the sacrifice, the wood, and the stones. Then he repeated the order a second time: "Do that again." Then again a third time: "Do that again." Twelve barrels of water drenched the sacrifice, soaked the wood, ran down through the rocks forming the altar, and filled to the brim a deep trench dug around the altar.

Should anyone suggest that a fire could have been made from a hidden spark from underneath the wood or some similar devious device? Elijah forestalled any such speculation by inundating the entire site with so much water that the whole altar was virtually swimming in the filled trench that surrounded it.

Then he prayed a simple prayer:

> O LORD God of Abraham, Isaac, and Jacob, prove today that you are God in Israel and that I am your servant. Prove that I have done all this at your command. O LORD, answer me! Answer me so these people will know that

you, O LORD, are God and that you have brought them
back to yourself. (1 Kings 18:36–37)

And the fire fell. A mighty, heavenly fire, not just a bolt of lightning, for it consumed the meat offering; it consumed the soaking-
wet wood on which the bull was resting; it consumed the very
stones of the altar, the dirt trench, and the water in the trench. The
whole site just went up in a white roaring blaze of smoke and hiss-
ing steam! When it was over, there wasn't a thing left except a God-
scorched oval on the rocky hilltop where the altar and sacrifice had
been.

All the people cried out with a single voice, "The LORD—he is
God! Yes, the LORD is God!" (1 Kings 18:39).

Elijah, obviously, never doubted it.

To read this story about Elijah, go to 1 Kings 18:16–46.

The Night Stalker

Nehemiah Takes a Walk to View the Walls of Jerusalem

NOT MANY of us would take a walk in a bad neighborhood or
through the streets of a war-torn city at night. But Nehemiah
did. Lest we think Nehemiah had a death wish, we need to know his
story. Let's start with his resume:

Nehemiah: displaced man of Israel, during the time of
　　　Israel's exile
Occupation: cupbearer (butler) to Artaxerxes, King of
　　　Persia
Location: Susa

Not only did he have a great job, Nehemiah also was well liked by his boss. He had it made. But after one of his brothers told him about the dangerous conditions of the city of Jerusalem with its broken walls, Nehemiah had a strong sense of compassion for his people in that area. A wall was usually the first line of defense for a people. Without it, enemies could swoop in and slaughter. The former Jewish exiles who had returned to live in Jerusalem were defenseless.

Nehemiah took the matter to God in prayer, but not content to just pray or listen to the reports of others, he determined to do something about the situation. He would go and rebuild that wall!

In a position of service like his, Nehemiah couldn't just pack and leave. He had to have the permission of the king. But even a well-liked servant couldn't simply express his problems. He had to wait for the king to ask. Amazingly, King Artaxerxes asked Nehemiah why he looked sad. This was the God-shaped opening Nehemiah needed. He requested permission to return to Israel and help rebuild the city.

The king would have been within his rights to refuse. But instead, he gave his permission as well as letters that would guarantee Nehemiah safe passage all the way to Judah. For the building supplies he would need, another letter was given for the royal forester.

"Anything else you need, Nehemiah?"

"How about some troops to go with me?"

"Done."

This amazing bounty was made possible by the Lord's favor. The book of Proverbs explains why: "The king's heart is a stream of water in the hand of the LORD; he turns it wherever he will" (Proverbs 21:1 ESV). So off to Jerusalem he went, fully provided for.

Then one night, some dark figures lurked in the shadows of the dilapidated wall. They silently walked over and under stones, in and out of gates. Nehemiah's secret night-stalking SWAT team examined the wall carefully, taking inventory. Nehemiah must have grieved over every broken brick, every sign of the destruction that had occurred decades previously when Babylon sacked the city (see 2 Kings 25:10).

By the light of day, Nehemiah set out to convince the city leaders to rebuild the wall. After Nehemiah explained how God was with him, "They replied, 'Let us start rebuilding.' So they began this good work" (Nehemiah 2:18 NIV).

Later, other dark figures were lurking in the shadows—enemies who mocked and ridiculed them. But Nehemiah was confident that God would continue to meet their needs and bring this project to a successful conclusion.

Read about Nehemiah's night walk around the wall in Nehemiah 2:11–20.

The Perils of Pride

Hezekiah Provides a Treasury Tour That Leads to Trouble

IT'S HUMAN NATURE to want to keep up with the Joneses and show off a bit—especially when we have some cool new gadget or the latest status symbol. But sometimes showing off can prove perilous, as Hezekiah discovered.

Hezekiah was the king of Judah—part of David's family line. The best thing that could be said about Hezekiah was that he trusted God. "There was no one like him among all the kings of Judah, either before him or after him. . . . And the LORD was with him; he was successful in whatever he undertook" (2 Kings 18:5, 7 NIV)— this was the kind of sound bite to assure him a spot on the History Channel. He was successful in battle, daring to defy the powerful king of Assyria and being saved from the horrors of a slaughter by the arrival of one angel who wiped out a huge portion of the Assyrian army (read about that in "A Good King Cleans House," p. 133). God even gave him a longer life when a deathly illness threatened.

You can almost sense the *but* coming. But . . . even successful, God-fearing kings have weaknesses. Hezekiah's weakness became apparent when envoys from Babylon arrived to check out Jerusalem. Merodach-Baladan, a prince of Babylon, arrived in town bearing a gift for the newly recovered king of Judah. While that might sound like good PR among nations, you'll see in a minute why that was dangerous.

Grateful for the gift, Hezekiah decided to give his guests a tour of the treasury. See all of the lovely things we have? Gold, silver, and spices. And over here is the armory—look at our cache of weapons. This tour was nothing if not thorough. The Babylonian ambassadors received an eyeful.

But there was a prophet in town also—Isaiah. After asking the king about the nature of the Babylonians' visit, Isaiah had bad news for the proud king: one day the Babylonians would swoop in and take everything from Israel, including the people. This calamity would not take place until after the days of Hezekiah.

We have only to read 2 Kings 25 to see the fulfillment of this prophecy. While Hezekiah died, still feeling peaceful and secure, a future generation paid the price of that terrible treasury tour.

For more about this story, read Isaiah 39.

Captain Underpants

Jeremiah Uses Dirty Underwear to Condemn Israel's Actions

BEING A PROPHET during the often turbulent Old Testament times was not easy. And for a prophet like Jeremiah, life was sometimes more than a little hairy. You see, God often had unusual requests for his prophets (see "Just a Stone's Throw Away," p. 57). He liked using an object lesson to show his people how he felt when they disobeyed him. And one of those lessons involved Jeremiah's buying a new "linen belt" (Jeremiah 13:1 NIV), which in Bible language means underwear.

That's right. *Underwear.* This was not a strong hint to Jeremiah to spruce up his wardrobe or the kind of warning a parent would give to get a kid to avoid leaving the house with ragged underwear. Note the words *object lesson* in the paragraph above. Like the crime-fighting hero of the Captain Underpants series by Dav Pilkey, underwear would become the symbol in the fight against evil. So Jeremiah was to buy a linen undergarment and wear it, but not wash it.

Wow. Dirty-underwear alert. Perhaps you're wondering now why God would place his prophet in such an unhygienic state. Although the text never says how long Jeremiah wore the dirty undergarment, wear it he did.

Once Jeremiah complied with the request, God had another command: go to Perath, hundreds of miles away, and hide the undergarment in a crevice.

All righty then!

With that done, God told Jeremiah to return to the area and dig up the belt.

We're having some fun now, huh, Jeremiah?

What happens when you bury an unwashed garment in a rocky crevice? It gets ruined, that's what. Who knows how filthy and germ-ridden the undergarment looked when Jeremiah took it out of the crevice. It was completely unusable now. God had a message for Israel through this garment: "Just like this I will ruin the great pride of both Judah and Jerusalem. These evil people, who refuse to listen to Me, who walk in the stubbornness of their own hearts, and who have followed other gods to serve and worship—they will be like this underwear, of no use whatsoever" (Jeremiah 13:9–10 HCSB).

No doubt about it—sin has consequences.

To read more about this story, see Jeremiah 13:1–11.

Just a Stone's
Throw Away

*Jeremiah Throws His Scroll into the River as an Object
Lesson*

THIS IS A RATHER droll role for a scroll.
Most writers would like to see their words go far and be
read in faraway places. Jeremiah was no exception. He wrote out an
elaborate series of prophetic poems about Babylon (you can read
these in Jeremiah 50–51) and then entrusted them into the hands of
a fellow Israelite named Seraiah, who happened to be going, at that
moment, to distant Babylon. It seemed an opportune occasion.

But the bearer of the scroll with Jeremiah's written work on it
was no doubt puzzled by the accompanying instructions. It wasn't
the usual authorial patter about being careful not to lose any of the
manuscript, and not to get it wet, and not to let it roll into a camp-
fire, etc.

"When you get to Babylon," Jeremiah told him in no uncertain
terms, "read this aloud. It explains all the evil that will some day
come upon Babylon. Then after you read the conclusion, roll up the
scroll, tie a stone to it securely, and throw it way out into the middle
of the Euphrates River. In the shocked silence that follows your odd
act, pronounce clearly: 'Thus shall Babylon sink, to rise no more,
because of the disaster that I am bringing upon her, and they shall
become exhausted'" (Jeremiah 51:64 ESV).

Jeremiah was no stranger to odd object lessons. God had him do many strange things that were visual aids to the prophetic words he announced (see "Captain Underpants," p. 55). God knew that sometimes people needed more than just words; they needed to *see* the point of those words. In case the people didn't understand his words, such as "Because of the wrath of the LORD [Babylon] shall not be inhabited but shall be an utter desolation" (Jeremiah 50:13), or "Wild beasts shall dwell with hyenas in Babylon, and ostriches shall dwell in her. She shall never again have people, nor be inhabited for all generations" (Jeremiah 50:39), or "How Babylon is taken" (Jeremiah 51:41), God sent an object lesson, saying in so many words, "Take the scroll and toss it in the river to show what I mean by 'utter desolation' and 'not inhabited' and 'taken.'"

And true to Jeremiah's prediction, Babylon did indeed fall to rise no more. (Looking for Babylon on a map? You won't find it.) The book of Daniel tells us the rest of the story. Mysterious handwriting appeared on the wall of Belshazzar's palace, warning "your kingdom is divided and given to the Medes and Persians." True to that prophecy, and the words of many prophets before (including Jeremiah), "that very night Belshazzar the Chaldean [Babylonian] king was killed. And Darius the Mede received the kingdom" (Daniel 5:28, 30–31 ESV).

To read more about this incident, see Jeremiah 51:59–64.

A Scroll with Honey and a Side Order of Sleep

Ezekiel Eats a Scroll and Lies on His Side

GOD TOLD EZEKIEL to do some pretty bizarre things. If behavior were any warrant for truth, we'd have to wonder about this guy. The things Ezekiel did in public were so wacky, so completely unexpected, that people today would confidently assume he was completely off his rocker.

One of the many symbolic acts he was commanded to perform involved a papyrus scroll. God told his prophet: "'Son of man, eat this scroll I am giving you and fill your stomach with it.' So I ate it, and it tasted as sweet as honey in my mouth. He then said to me: 'Son of man, go now to the house of Israel and speak my words to them'" (Ezekiel 3:3–4 NIV).

Ezekiel's next task was to take a clay tablet and create a miniature battle scene. First, he drew the city of Jerusalem on the clay. Then he erected siege works and built a ramp and set up camps and battering rams. Then what was his job? To lay down on his left side facing the tablet for exactly 390 days. Why 390 days? God explained, "I have assigned you the same number of days as the years of their sin. So for 390 days you will bear the sin of the house of Israel" (Ezekiel 4:5).

When that time was completed, Ezekiel had to get up, turn over, and lie down again—this time on his right side. He rolled up his sleeve, bared his arm, and denounced the tablet (the city of Jerusalem) in a loud voice, prophesying. He did that for forty days, symbolic of the forty years of Judah's punishment.

People walking by on the street must have found it puzzling, amusing, and strange beyond comprehension to see this eccentric man lying on one side, yelling at a brick, and threatening it with menacing prophecies for over a year. To be sure, the prophet was communicating something of great significance, but what did it mean?

Ezekiel did get to eat during this time, so not to worry. Wheat, barley, beans, lentils, millet, and spelt (yum!) were the ingredients he could use to make bread during the 390-day prophecy. But don't ask what kind of fuel he used to cook each day's small meal . . . you don't want to know. (Oh, okay; if you insist on the details, it's all there in Ezekiel 4:9–16. Didn't I tell you that you wouldn't want to know?)

Why did God prescribe such radical bizarre behavior to communicate his word? Ezekiel had been warned:

> You are not being sent to a people of obscure speech and difficult language, but to the house of Israel—not to many peoples of obscure speech and difficult language, whose words you cannot understand. Surely if I had sent you to them, they would have listened to you. But the house of Israel is not willing to listen to you because they are not willing to listen to me, for the whole house of Israel is hardened and obstinate. But I will make you as unyielding and hardened as they are. I will make your forehead like the hardest stone, harder than flint. Do not be afraid of them or terrified by them, though they are a rebellious house. (Ezekiel 3:5–9)

Apparently unusual times of stubborn apostasy require unusual means of reproof.

To read more, see Ezekiel 3:1–15; 4:1–17.

Unusual Behavior of God's Prophets

Prophet	Unusual Behavior
Jeremiah	Burying a loincloth in a far-off country, then retrieving it after it was ruined to show that Israel and Judah will likewise be ruined (Jeremiah 13:1–11) Living without wife, children; not mourning or feasting with others to show the disaster that was to fall on Israel (Jeremiah 16:1–13) Wearing a yoke over his neck to show that Israel must submit to the Babylonian empire (Jeremiah 27:1–15)
Ezekiel	Laid on his side 430 days (390 on left, 40 on right) in front of a model of Jerusalem; ate food cooked over excrement; shaved his head and burned the hair—all to show the coming siege, ruin, and sack of Jerusalem (Ezekiel 4–5) Acted out the role of an exile to show the fate of the people of Jerusalem (Ezekiel 12) Did not grieve over the death of his wife to show that God will not grieve over the destruction of Jerusalem (Ezekiel 24:15–27)
Hosea	Married an unfaithful wife to show how Israel was unfaithful to God (Hosea 1; 3)
Jonah	Fled his commission to prophesy against Nineveh; swallowed by a great fish to show the futility of evading God's will (Jonah 1–2)

PROPHET	UNUSUAL BEHAVIOR
John the Baptist	Lived in the wilderness, eating as a scavenger to show that the wealth of the priests was not a sign of holiness, and also to reveal himself as a prophet of God (Matthew 3:1–12, Mark 1:1–8; Luke 3:1–17)
Agabus	Took Paul's belt and tied up his hands and feet to prophesy what awaited Paul in Jerusalem (Acts 21:10–11)

Hair Today, Gone Tomorrow

Ezekiel Uses an Extreme Haircut to Get to the Root of Israel's Sin

WATCHING EZEKIEL'S prophetic antics during the Jewish exile in Babylon was like watching a play. The audience, the people of Israel, never knew what God would tell him to do next. And for the most part, they didn't like what they saw.

The next act in the play involved a haircut. Ezekiel was told to take a sword and shave his head and beard. In those days, a man wouldn't do such a thing unless he was in mourning. For Ezekiel to appear in public like that would have been humiliating. But Ezekiel didn't have the kind of prophetic ministry that allowed for much pride. So his hair today was gone tomorrow.

So far so good. Next, Ezekiel was to take the hair and divide it into three sections. One third was to be burned. Another third was to be struck with a sword. The last third was to be thrown to the wind. In addition, God had something in mind for some of the strands of hair in the third group. Ezekiel was to stash them away in his clothing. Yet some of them were to be burned as well.

So what did this all add up to? The hair symbolized what was in store for the people still left in Jerusalem—utter humiliation and devastation. A third would die during the siege and burning of Jerusalem. Another third would die at the hands of enemy invaders. Still another group would be scattered through exile. But of the final group, some would go through the fires of judgment, while some others would die in exile.

And what of the hairs in Ezekiel's clothing? That remnant of hair represented the remnant of the faithful whom God planned to save.

This prophecy of doom came about due to Israel's rebellion over decades and under various idol-worshiping kings. Prophets like Isaiah and Jeremiah prophesied of the coming destruction of Jerusalem and the exile the people would suffer. In fact, Isaiah had this chilling prophecy:

> In that day the LORD will whistle for the army of southern Egypt and for the army of Assyria. They will swarm around you like flies and bees. They will come in vast hordes and settle in the fertile areas and also in the desolate valleys, caves, and thorny places. In that day the Lord will hire a "razor" from beyond the Euphrates River—the king of Assyria—and use it to shave off everything: your land, your crops, and your people. (Isaiah 7:18–20 NLT)

In a way Ezekiel was a visual reminder of this prophecy, which did come to pass (see 2 Kings 25).

Find more about Ezekiel's unusual haircut in Ezekiel 5:1–6.

A Wife Unmourned

Ezekiel Is Asked by God Not to Mourn the Death of His Wife

EVERY ONCE in a while some committee of psychologists or stress managers will put together a scale on which they place various sources of stress and anxiety in relation to one another. Losing a job always places high on the list, along with divorce, moving from one city to another, the death of a parent, and as many as a dozen other known causes of stress.

But one of the most stressful and painful experiences for most people is the loss of a mate. When people lose the one with whom they've become "one flesh," as the Bible expresses it, the grief is intense. There are no words for the loss. To not grieve would be unthinkable.

Every culture has traditional mourning customs—accepted means by which the bereaved can express their deep pain and loss. Ezekiel's generation had their customs too. Yet one day God told him, "Son of man, with one blow I am about to take away from you the delight of your eyes. Yet do not lament or weep or shed any tears" (Ezekiel 24:16 NIV).

The unthinkable tragedy indeed occurred; several hours later Ezekiel's wife died. He complied with the Lord's admonition to be silent about it and show no outward signs of mourning, not even tears. His neighbors were evidently nonplussed. "What are you doing, Ezekiel? What does this mean that your wife has been taken from you and you appear indifferent?"

God prepared him with an answer, a prophetic speaking-for-God in which the Lord showed that he, too, has had to deal with the loss of his beloved—his people and his sanctuary in Jerusalem.

> The word of the LORD came to me: Say to the house of Israel, "This is what the Sovereign LORD says: I am about to desecrate my sanctuary—the stronghold in which you take pride, the delight of your eyes, the object of your affection. The sons and daughters you left behind will fall by the sword. And you will do as I have done. You will not cover the lower part of your face or eat the customary food [of mourners]. You will keep your turbans on your heads and your sandals on your feet. You will not mourn or weep but will waste away because of your sins and groan among yourselves. Ezekiel will be a sign to you; you will do just as he has done. When this happens, you will know that I am the Sovereign LORD." (Ezekiel 24:20–24)

The sacking of the city, the destruction of his temple, and the slaughter of his beloved children who lived there—before it ever happened, God knew and determined that it would. He steeled himself against feeling pity for his beloved people for he knew they *had* to go through this purgation. What he told Ezekiel to do was simply to model the Lord's own feelings and controlled expression of grief.

This incident is found in Ezekiel 24:15–27.

Food Fight

Daniel and His Friends Follow Dietary Laws and Wind Up in a Food Fight

THE PEOPLE OF ISRAEL had a stormy history. One of the darkest periods of their history involved the destruction of the temple and the walls of Jerusalem when the Babylonian army invaded Judah. The result was exile for the people of Jerusalem.

But even in dark periods, light can be found. When the Israelites were dragged away from their homeland, Daniel, Hananiah, Mishael, and Azariah were among them. (Most of us know the latter three as Shadrach, Meshach, and Abednego—the Babylonian names given to them.) These young men would be a source of light to their enemies. Food was the catalyst.

Once the people of Israel were taken to Babylon, the Babylonian king Nebuchadnezzar decided to allow a group of Israelite young men to become part of his court. To join this three-year program of study, there were a few requirements to make the cut. These young men had to be the cream of the crop—related to royalty, physically attractive, well rounded, and brilliant. Not too hard, right?

The program included a full "tuition, room, and board" grant to study Babylonian language and literature and receive food and wine from the king's own table. It sounded pretty sweet on the surface. But you know what happens when you eat too many sweets.

The four bright young men, Daniel, Shadrach, Meshach, and Abednego, made the admissions cut. Instead of puffing themselves

66

up and forgetting where they came from, they determined to retain a part of their culture. And a big part of their culture was honoring God by obeying certain dietary laws. As Daniel explained, they did not want to defile themselves by eating the king's food. The food fight was on.

But even in their resolve, Daniel and his friends showed respect to the Babylonian officials. They asked the man in charge of supplying the food and drink for permission to stick to their own dietary plan—eating vegetables and drinking water. "But the king will have my head if you don't follow his orders to eat his food!" the official protested. Daniel asked for a compromise: after ten days he could see how their health compared to the others in the program.

The wait was on. Would the vegetables-and-water regimen prove the ticket? The answer was—yes! Daniel and his friends wound up looking even better than those who stuck to the king's rich diet. God honored their desire to honor him above all. In the years to come, they would be tested again and again. But their faith in God stood the test of time.

To get more details about this story, read Daniel 1.

Out of His Mind

Failing to Honor God Has Dire Consequences for Nebuchad-nezzar

THE OLD SONG "My Way" was one of Frank Sinatra's signature songs, one that speaks of shouldering one's own way in life. The song's gutsy refrain, "I did it my way," could have been King Nebuchadnezzar's signature motto as well.

If Nebuchadnezzar had written his memoirs, he would have included the following information: "King of Babylon; owner of massive wealth; commander of an unstoppable army that conquered the known world; establisher of one of the seven wonders of the ancient world—the beautiful hanging gardens." Achieving such heights of power can go to a guy's head.

One day, while admiring all that he had achieved—all that he did *his* way—Nebuchadnezzar was troubled by a dream. Perhaps he should have read up on Pharaoh and the story of Joseph. He turned to his astrologers for answers. But they could not interpret the dream.

There was one person left to try: Belteshazzar, also known as Daniel—a man taken during the invasion of Judah. Daniel had risen in authority in Nebuchadnezzar's court and had an air of being in touch with the gods, according to Nebuchadnezzar, who knew little about the God of Israel.

So the king told Daniel his dream. In the dream, he saw a huge tree with ripe fruit—enough for the animals and birds to come and eat their fill. But then he heard a voice ordering the tree to be cut down, leaving the stump of the tree. The voice came from a shining being who seemed to come from the sky.

And then the shining being gave the most chilling pronouncement of all: "Let him live with the animals among the plants of the earth. Let his mind be changed from that of a man and let him be given the mind of an animal, till seven times pass by for him" (Daniel 4:15–16 NIV).

Daniel succeeded where the king's astrologers failed. The tree was Nebuchadnezzar, Daniel explained. Like the tree, he was about to be cut down. He would wander around like an animal for a time decided by God. Once he acknowledged God instead of his own pride, his kingdom would be given back to him.

Imagine having to say those words to the most powerful king in the world! Although we don't know what happened two seconds after Daniel's interpretation, what we do know is that Daniel's words came to pass.

Nebuchadnezzar suddenly heard a voice announcing that now was the time when his kingdom would be taken from him. Before he knew it, he was behaving like an animal—crawling around on the grass like the cattle of the field, his hair wild. Gone was the powerful, stately king of Babylon. He remained like that—completely out of his mind—until he finally offered praise to God—the true King of the world.

After a time, Nebuchadnezzar returned to his beautiful palace. But he continued to praise God. Whether he remained a true worshiper of God is unknown, but at least he realized one thing: God knew how to humble "those who walk in pride" (Daniel 4:37).

For more about Nebuchadnezzar's transformation, read Daniel 4.

STRANGE DREAMS AND VISIONS

Many people in the Bible had strange encounters with God through dreams or visions. These dreams and visions were not just limited to prophets. God spoke to kings, fathers, and others through dreams. Here are some of the dreams and visions and what they meant.

PERSON	VISION	INTERPRETATION OR FULFILLMENT OF THE VISION
Abram (Genesis 15:12–21)	In the midst of a heavy sleep, Abram found himself surrounded by thick darkness. He saw "a smoking fire pot and a flaming torch" (v. 17 HCSB) which passed between the sacrifices Abram offered to God.	The fire pot and flaming torch were a visual representation of God's presence.
Jacob (Genesis 28:10–19)	Jacob saw angels ascending and descending a stairway leading to heaven. He also heard the voice of God.	Through this dream, God promised to give Jacob's descendants land. This came to pass in the book of Joshua when Israel moved into Canaan.
Joseph (Genesis 37:5–11)	In Joseph's first dream, a sheaf of wheat belonging to Joseph stood while other sheaves of wheat— those belonging to his brothers—encircled it and bowed to it. In a second dream, the sun, moon, and eleven stars bowed to him.	Joseph's brothers and father would someday bow down to him. It came to pass when Joseph became the second-in-command in Egypt (see also Genesis 42–46).

PERSON	VISION	INTERPRETATION OR FULFILLMENT OF THE VISION
Pharaoh (Genesis 41)	In the first dream, seven fat cows followed by seven painfully thin cows exited the Nile River. The seven thin cows ate the fat cows. In the second, seven abundant heads of grain grew on a stalk and were eaten by seven shriveled heads of grain.	Seven years of prosperity would be followed by seven years of famine. Almost immediately, the dream came to pass.
Moses (Exodus 3:1–3)	Moses saw a bush clearly on fire but not consumed by the flames.	This bush was God's way of getting Moses' attention. God often used fire to show his presence. (See also Exodus 13:21, where God appeared as a pillar of fire.)
A Midianite soldier (Judges 7:8–25)	In the dream, a loaf of barley bread rolled down a hill and destroyed the tents of the Midianites.	Gideon and his three hundred men would be victorious over the Midianite horde. The dream was fulfilled almost immediately after the dream.
Solomon (1 Kings 3:5–15)	The Lord appeared to Solomon through a dream.	Solomon was given the wisdom he asked for and the riches he did not. Almost immediately, his wisdom became apparent (see also 1 Kings 3:16–28).
Micaiah (1 Kings 22:19–23)	Micaiah saw the Lord on a throne having a conversation with the angels. In this vision, Micaiah heard the Lord tell of his plan to allow King Ahab to be lied to and defeated.	Even though he disguised himself, Ahab was killed in battle just as Micaiah predicted (see also 1 Kings 22:29–39).

Person	Vision	Interpretation or Fulfillment of the Vision
Isaiah (Isaiah 6)	Isaiah saw the Lord on a throne. Above the throne were six-winged seraphim.	This was Isaiah's call to the prophetic ministry.
Ezekiel (Ezekiel 1)	Ezekiel saw cherubim with four faces controlling wheels bisected by other wheels. The cherubim had four wings and four faces. One face was that of a man, one was a lion, one resembled an ox, and the last an eagle. Ezekiel later saw on a sapphire throne "a figure like that of a man . . . he looked like glowing metal" (Ezekiel 1:26–27 NIV).	This was Ezekiel's call to the prophetic ministry. The vision powerfully symbolized God's presence and authority.
Ezekiel (Ezekiel 8–11)	Ezekiel saw a vision of the corruption of the temple of Jerusalem. He also saw an idol of jealousy. At the end of the vision, the glory of the Lord left the temple.	The statue was an idol dedicated to the false god Asherah. Because of idolatry and continued rebellion, God would allow his people to be scattered and their city destroyed.

PERSON	VISION	INTERPRETATION OR FULFILLMENT OF THE VISION
Ezekiel (Ezekiel 37:1–14)	Ezekiel saw a valley filled with dry bones. When told to prophesy to the bones, skin and muscles returned to the bones. But the bones held no life. When told to prophesy again, life entered the bones and they became a living army.	The bones represented Israel during the exile.
Nebuchadnezzar (Daniel 2)	In his dream, Nebuchadnezzar saw a huge statue with a head of gold, a chest and arms of silver, a stomach and thighs of bronze, and legs of iron. But the statue's toes were made of clay. A rock smashed the statue.	The dream showed the conquering kingdoms of the world. The gold represented the Babylonians; the silver, the Medes and Persians; the bronze, the Greeks; and the iron, the Romans. But the fifth kingdom, mentioned in Daniel 2:44–45, is the kingdom of God formed out of people on earth. This is the "rock" that broke the statue.
Nebuchadnezzar (Daniel 4)	The dream featured a tree with abundant fruit. Birds and animals fed from it. But a voice from heaven ordered that the tree be cut down, leaving only a stump.	Nebuchadnezzar was the tree. After a period of insanity, he was restored to his kingdom.

PERSON	VISION	INTERPRETATION OR FULFILLMENT OF THE VISION
Daniel (Daniel 7)	Daniel saw four beasts: a lion with the wings of an eagle, a bear chewing on three ribs, a leopard with four bird wings, and a beast with iron teeth and ten horns that destroyed all it touched.	The first beast was Babylon; the second, the Medes and Persians; and the third was Greece. The fourth beast represented the Romans.
Daniel (Daniel 8)	In this vision, a ram with two horns seemed all-powerful until defeated by a goat with one horn. When the horn of the goat was broken, four new horns grew. Out of these horns came a smaller horn.	The ram was the empire of the Medes and the Persians. The goat represented the Greeks, especially Alexander the Great (the large horn). Four nations would grow out of this nation. But yet another ruler would arise who would cause great destruction.
Daniel (Daniel 10)	Daniel saw a man "dressed in linen, whose waist was girded with a belt of pure gold of Uphaz. His body also was like beryl, his face had the appearance of lightning, his eyes were like flaming torches, his arms and feet like the gleam of polished bronze" (Daniel 10:5–6 NASB).	This angel was sent to explain a previous vision of Daniel.

PERSON	VISION	INTERPRETATION OR FULFILLMENT OF THE VISION
Daniel (Daniel 11–12)	In this vision, Daniel learned that a mighty king in the south will fight against a northern king. This southern king will invade Israel and destroy many people, but will eventually be defeated. Two men stood by the river talking about a time of persecution when the regular sacrifices cease.	This was a vision of the end times.
Joel (Joel 1)	A swarm of locusts devoured everything in the land.	The locusts represented God's judgment against unfaithful Israel.
Amos (Amos 7:1–6)	Amos saw a swarm of locusts.	A famine would come and the people would starve.
Amos (Amos 7:7–9)	Amos saw a plumb line.	God used the plumb line to measure how "off plumb" the people were. They did not keep his commandments.
Amos (Amos 8)	Amos saw a basket of ripe fruit.	The basket represented Israel, who was ripe for destruction.
Zechariah (Zechariah 1:7–17)	Zechariah saw a man on a red horse near a stand of myrtle trees. In his vision he heard a voice speaking.	The man on the horse was the angel of the Lord.

Person	Vision	Interpretation or Fulfillment of the Vision
Zechariah (Zechariah 1:18–21)	Zechariah saw four horns and four craftsmen.	The four horns were the nations that conquered Judah and Jerusalem: Assyria, Egypt, Babylonia, and the combined Medes and Persians. The four craftsmen were Egypt, Babylonia, Persia, and Greece.
Zechariah (Zechariah 2)	Zechariah saw a man with a measuring line.	After the boundaries of Israel were marked, God would restore his people.
Zechariah (Zechariah 3)	Zechariah saw the high priest, Joshua, standing before the angel of the Lord. Satan, the accuser, also stood before the Lord, condemning the priest. The priest was told of a Branch to come.	Joshua represented Israel after the exile. The Branch was the Messiah.
Zechariah (Zechariah 4)	Zechariah saw a golden lampstand on top of which was a bowl with seven lights and seven channels to each light. Nearby stood two olive trees. Later Zechariah saw two olive branches.	The lampstand and bowl represented God. The olive trees represented the priesthood and the kingship of Israel. The two olive branches were Joshua (the priest) and Zerubbabel, the governor who helped rebuild the temple (see Ezra 3).
Zechariah (Zechariah 5:1–4)	Zechariah saw a flying scroll.	This was a curse that worked against commandment breakers.
Zechariah (Zechariah 5:5–11)	Zechariah saw a woman sitting in a basket. Two angels took the basket to Babylonia.	The woman symbolized sinful Israel. God would allow his people to be taken to Babylon to be cleansed of their sins.

Person	Vision	Interpretation or Fulfillment of the Vision
Zechariah (Zechariah 6:1–8)	Zechariah saw four chariots: one with red horses; one with black; one with white; and the last with dappled horses.	These were angels going forth at God's bidding.
Zechariah (Luke 1:11–17)	An angel of the Lord appeared to Zechariah, telling him that he would have a son who would make ready a people prepared for the Lord.	John the Baptist was born.
Joseph (Matthew 1:18–25)	Joseph saw the angel of the Lord, who told him not to "divorce" Mary, who carried the Son of God in her womb.	Joseph married Mary.
Joseph (Matthew 2:13–15)	Joseph saw the angel of the Lord once again, who warned him to take the child Jesus and his mother into Egypt.	Joseph obeyed and headed to Egypt, thus protecting the infant Jesus from Herod's slaughter of the babies in Bethlehem
Joseph (Matthew 2:19–23)	Joseph saw the angel of the Lord a third time, who told him that the family could now leave Egypt.	Joseph took his family to Nazareth in Galilee.
The wife of Pilate (Matthew 27:19)	Although the details of the dream are not given, Pilate's wife evidently knew that Jesus was an innocent man.	Pilate's wife begged Pilate to have nothing to do with condemning Jesus to death. But Pilate did not heed his wife's words.

PERSON	VISION	INTERPRETATION OR FULFILLMENT OF THE VISION
Paul (2 Corinthians 12:1–6)	Paul saw a vision of "the third heaven" (V.2 CEV) where he heard many things he could not express.	Like the apostle John and prophets like Isaiah and Ezekiel, Paul saw a vision of God.
John (Revelation 1–3)	John began his end-times visions with "someone 'like a son of man'" (Revelation 1:13 NIV) as well as seven lampstands.	The son of man was Jesus who discussed the seven lampstands—the churches in Asia Minor.
John (Revelation 4)	John saw one on a throne who "had the appearance of jasper and carnelian" (V.3 ESV). Before the throne were twenty-four elders. He also saw four creatures with many eyes. One was like a lion, another like an ox. The third had a man's face, while the fourth was like an eagle.	This vision of heaven showed twenty-four leaders of believers or angels worshiping God. The creatures were probably cherubim like those seen by Ezekiel (see Ezekiel 1:10–14).
John (Revelation 5–20)	The rest of the book of Revelation are John's visions of the end times.	However one interprets them, these visions will be fulfilled because they are God's words.

PERSON	VISION	INTERPRETATION OR FULFILLMENT OF THE VISION
John (Revelation 21)	John saw the new Jerusalem and a vision of the Bride of Christ. During the vision, he learned that no sorrow or death would occur in the city. The city had twelve gates, one for each of the apostles. It had streets of gold and walls made of gems.	This was a vision of the new heaven.
John (Revelation 22:1–6)	John saw the water of life and trees with abundant fruit.	This Eden-like vision is a fitting bookend to the Genesis account where mankind failed in obedience. Here, "no longer will there be any curse" (V.3 NIV).

PART THREE
Sinister Schemes

Scheming for Sons

Lot's "Family Values" Lead to Incest

IF YOU READ "Lot's Family Values" (p. 28) and Genesis 19:1–29, you know that Lot's family could have made the rounds of the talk-show circuit (had talk shows existed at that time). But some stories end, as a famous T.S. Eliot poem says, "not with a bang but a whimper." The story of Lot, Abraham's nephew, ends with the whimper of two infants who had the distinction of being Lot's sons *and* grandsons at the same time. How is that possible? Let's start at the beginning.

Lot had a wife, two daughters, and two future sons-in-law—a fine family. He also thought he had a long future in beautiful, downtown Sodom in the fertile Jordan plain. But that dream died when God decided to destroy Sodom and its twin city, Gomorrah, due to the unending evil of the inhabitants.

God graciously sent two angels to warn Lot to flee to the mountains with his family and with any others who wished to become part of his family. His daughters' fiancés foolishly decided not to heed the warning. After an awful night in which Lot offered to send his daughters to slake the lust of the men of the city rather than offer his guests (the angels), the family finally escaped. But during the escape, Lot's wife came to an unfortunate end as a pillar of salt. Lot and his daughters barely made it to the mountains before the fiery destruction of both cities and the surrounding plain.

How does a family start life over after a disaster of that magnitude? Well, Lot's daughters decided to start over with children by the only man in the vicinity—their father. Mix a little alcohol with a man grieving the deaths of his wife and his dreams, and what do you have? A recipe for trouble concocted by two desperate sisters. First, the oldest daughter gave Lot enough wine to get him drunk enough to sleep with her. On the following day, the younger daughter followed her sister's example. Meanwhile, Lot had no idea what happened.

Both sisters became pregnant and conceived sons. These sons, Moab and Ben-Ammi, later became the ancestors of some of Israel's bitterest enemies: the Moabites and the Ammonites.

Some sins have long-lasting consequences.

This sad saga can be found in Genesis 19:30–38.

Cooking Up a Plot

Jacob and Rebekah Cook Up a Recipe for Betrayal

SOME FAMILIES are so dysfunctional that one does not need a psychology degree to pinpoint the issues. They're just obvious. Isaac's family was such a family.

Isaac married and had twin sons. But soon the family was split in half due to favoritism. Isaac favored his firstborn son, Esau—the rough-and-tumble man of the outdoors. Isaac's wife, Rebekah, favored her younger son, the quieter, indoorsy, helps-out-in-the-kitchen kind of guy, Jacob, which means "trickster." The name was an apt choice, as this story proves.

Before we get into it, let's review. Because Esau was born seconds before Jacob, he had the birthright of the firstborn. This usually meant having a double portion of anything inherited through the father. But during a hungry moment in Esau's life, Jacob offered to give him food in exchange for Esau's birthright (see "Broth for a Birthright," p. 33). The following story shows how Esau's actions came back to haunt him; it involves another instance in which food plays a part in this birthright saga.

The time had come for Isaac to bestow his blessing on his first-born son. Before giving it, he had one request: that Esau bring him some wild game that Isaac loved. Rebekah overheard this request and determined that her favorite, Jacob, get the blessing instead. They came up with a scheme that Niccolò Machiavelli (the political advocate of the use of power and plots) would have approved of. To gain Isaac's blessing, and therefore the birthright, they had to fool old Isaac into believing that Jacob was Esau. This was not an impossible task, since the elderly Isaac could not see very well. All Jacob would have to do was wear a disguise, while Rebekah prepared a dish of the wild game Isaac loved best.

Because Esau was hairy and Jacob was smooth-skinned, Jacob donned goatskins on his arms and some of Esau's clothes on his back. So far so good. Jacob took the food to Isaac, even giving God the credit for its swift arrival. While Isaac's failing sight didn't allow him to discern Jacob's features, his ears could not be fooled. Still, Jacob talked his way out of an admission of the truth and gained the blessing.

Esau's later arrival and presentation of food caused Isaac to do a double take. But the blessing had already been given. Isaac could only cough up a second-best blessing for Esau: "Your dwelling will be away from the earth's richness, away from the dew of heaven above. You will live by the sword and you will serve your brother. But when you grow restless, you will throw his yoke from off your neck" (Genesis 27:39–40 NIV).

An enraged Esau vowed to kill Jacob. Once again Rebekah

came to Jacob's rescue, urging him to flee to his Uncle Laban's house. The story ends with the family estranged. Decades would pass before the brothers saw each other again. It just goes to show that betrayal, broth, birthrights, and blessings don't mix.

Read about Jacob's unsavory culinary plot in Genesis 27.

Shechem in Check

Dinah Sees the Sad Aftermath of Rape and Revenge

T HE OLD *Batman* animated series featured the antagonist Mr. Freeze, who always uttered the chillingly familiar proverb, "Revenge is a dish best served cold." The sons of Jacob would agree.

Jacob had four sons by his first wife, Leah: Reuben, Simeon, Levi, and Judah, plus two others through Leah's maid Zilpah. Jacob and Leah also had a daughter, Dinah. Although Jacob had six other sons, this sad episode in Dinah's life involves only the sons of Leah.

Dinah caught the eye of Shechem, the son of a Hivite named Hamor. Now, instead of going to Jacob to ask for her hand in marriage, Shechem decided to take what he wanted by force.

Although Jacob discovered what happened, he kept the news from Dinah's brothers for a time, undoubtedly knowing that the news would have an explosive impact on them. As far as they were concerned, the fact that Shechem later sought permission to marry

Dinah didn't make his actions right or even forgivable. In fact, Hamor's further suggestion that Jacob's family intermarry with his people galled Jacob's sons even further. But they weren't Jacob's sons for nothing! Proving that they inherited some of Jacob's trickster genes, they concocted a plan to get revenge on their sister's behalf.

The first step in the plan was to act friendly by suggesting that every man in the city be circumcised before any of the women of Israel were given to them as wives. God required all of Abraham's male descendants to be circumcised as a sign of their covenantal relationship with him. (See Genesis 17:10–14; Leviticus 12:3). By this sign, God's people were set apart from the other people groups in Canaan. Shechem and his father were among the first to perform the rite. After all, Hamor and the men in the area reasoned, they would gain all of the wealth of Jacob's family once the families blended.

The next step in the plan was to strike while all of the men rested and recovered from their circumcisions. Simeon and Levi attacked and killed every man in the city, including Hamor and Shechem. They then looted the city.

Although Jacob feared further revenge from the people in the area, his sons refused to show remorse for their actions. This sad story shows the problems of taking revenge. Perhaps that's why the apostle Paul wrote, "Beloved, never avenge yourselves, but leave it to the wrath of God, for it is written, 'Vengeance is mine, I will repay, says the Lord'" (Romans 12:19 ESV). In the case of Jacob's sons, revenge left everyone cold.

Read this sad story of revenge in Genesis 34.

Dealing with
a Dreamer

Joseph's Brothers Scheme to Get Rid of Him

JOSEPH WAS the obvious darling of his father. And just to make
sure that all of Joseph's eleven brothers knew he was the favorite,
Jacob made Joseph an incredibly beautiful, multicolored coat to
wear. No missing that.

Added to this, Joseph did little to endear himself to his brothers. He was a tattletale, ready with a bad report on his brothers
whenever the occasion arose. But what really annoyed the brothers
was their little brother's obnoxious habit of telling them about his
dreams—particularly when it involved them in a negative way.

His brothers hated him so much that they wouldn't even talk
to him.

One particular day, Joseph announced to his already-jealous
brothers: "Listen to this dream I had. We were all out in the field
gathering bundles of wheat. All of a sudden my bundle stood
straight up and your bundles circled around it and bowed to mine"
(Genesis 37:6–7 MSG).

The brothers (and remember there were eleven of them and
only one Joseph) stared at each other in amazement. Who was this
guy? Didn't he get it? "So! You're going to rule us? You're going to
boss us around?" they asked derisively. And, as the Bible states,

"they hated him more than ever because of his dreams and the way he talked" (Genesis 37:8).

Maybe life might have worked out differently for Joseph and his band of brothers if he had kept his dreams to himself. But whether Joseph was just oblivious to his brothers' feelings or incredibly obnoxious, he didn't stop. He had one more dream to share: "I dreamed another dream—the sun and moon and eleven stars bowed down to me" (Genesis 37:9).

This time, Joseph even told his father about his dream, and, finally, Jacob intervened. "What's with all this dreaming?" his father reprimanded him. "Am I and your mother and your brothers all supposed to bow down to you?" But while Jacob brooded about the situation, Joseph's brothers had had enough. Action was necessary to get rid of this dreamer.

The brothers got their opportunity a few days later. As they were out tending their father's flocks in the countryside, Jacob sent Joseph to check on them. Dutifully, Joseph tracked his brothers down at Dothan. But his brothers had spotted him approaching in the distance and quickly began plotting.

At first they suggested killing Joseph, throwing him in a cistern, and then claiming that a wild animal had attacked him. But Reuben persuaded his brothers not to kill Joseph but to just throw him into the cistern and leave him there. (Reuben secretly planned to go back later and rescue his little brother.) So when Joseph arrived, his brothers grabbed him, took off his fancy coat, and tossed him in the cistern. While his brothers were eating dinner, a group of Ishmaelites (also called Midianites) traveling from Gilead and heading to Egypt arrived.

What providence! Judah immediately suggested that rather than leaving their brother to die, why not trade Joseph to the Ishmaelites and have them take him to Egypt? After all, why should they carry the guilt of their brother's blood on their heads? The deal was struck, and off went Joseph to Egypt for twenty pieces of silver.

To cover up their evil scheme, the brothers killed a goat and then bloodied the multicolored coat as evidence that Joseph had indeed been killed by a wild animal.

Back they went to Jacob and presented the coat to him. The old man recognized it immediately and tore his clothes in grief. Although his sons and daughters tried to comfort him, Jacob would not be comforted. "I'll go to the grave mourning my son."

In the meantime, the Ishmaelites made a tidy profit off Joseph by selling him as a slave to Potiphar, one of the Pharaoh's officials. And while the brothers felt that they had accomplished their goal of getting rid of Joseph, little did they dream that one day their paths would cross again—and under vaguely familiar circumstances.

Who's the dreamer now?

The dreamer, his dreams, and what might have been his downfall are found in Genesis 37.

Gulled by the Gibeonites

The Gibeonites Resort to Trickery to Get a Treaty

BESIDES BEING the name of an aquatic bird, the word *gull* is also a verb that means "to deceive or cheat" according to the

American Heritage College Dictionary. But another offshoot of *gull* could be *Gibeonite*—"a person who deceives or cheats." Okay, perhaps that definition is not the *official* definition for *Gibeonite.* To see why it is apt, however, take a journey back in time to the conquest of the Promised Land as experienced by Joshua and the Israelites.

Canaan was called the Promised Land because God promised the Israelites that they would have it to live in (see Genesis 15:17–21; Joshua 1:1–9). But its then-current inhabitants didn't get the memo. So the people of Israel would have to fight their way through the land in order to claim it. In battle after battle in cities like Jericho and Ai, God helped the people vanquish their enemies.

So imagine how the non-Israelite people groups (the Gibeonites, Amorites, Hittites, Canaanites, etc.) felt as they watched the Hebrew "juggernaut" roll through the land, thanks to their unstoppable God. The people of Gibeon decided not to wait to be the next casualties. Since they couldn't outbattle the Israelites, perhaps they could outwit them.

The plan was this: a group of Gibeonites carrying a bag of stale bread and beat-up wineskins would be sent to meet with the leaders of Israel. They would give the leaders a sob story about traveling from a distant land and thus get them to make a treaty.

All worked according to plan. The Gibeonites, with downcast faces, traveled to the camp of the Israelites. With quivering voices, they described their long, arduous journey. "See our stale bread and old wineskins? Pity us. All we want is a treaty with you, Israel." They looked like the ultimate groupies.

Now Joshua, the leader of the Israelites, usually sought God's opinion. Not this time. This one seemed like a no-brainer. A treaty was made with the people of Gibeon almost immediately.

What a shock it must have been for Joshua and the Israelites to later discover that the people of Gibeon actually were near neighbors! Right around the corner, third garage on the left—you can't miss us. So the Israelites went to confront the Gibeonites, who had deceived them. But what could they do? They couldn't retaliate against a people with whom they had made a treaty.

Joshua had a better idea. The people of Gibeon would be the servants to the people of Israel from then on. The Gibeonites were flat out busted. They accepted Joshua's judgment, because at least it meant one good thing: they would get to live.

To learn more about the Gibeonites, read Joshua 9.

The Barber of Sorek

Samson Gets the Worst Haircut of His Life

GIOACHINO ROSSINI'S 1816 opera *The Barber of Seville* features the famed Figaro, who shaves one of the characters. While Rossini's opera was a comedy, tragedy was the result when a barber went to work in Samson's life.

During the period in Israel's history just before the advent of the kings, judges led the people of Israel against their enemies. A constant refrain in the book of Judges is, "The Israelites did evil in the eyes of the LORD" (Judges 2:11; 3:7, 12 NIV). But there was an antidote: "The LORD raised up judges, who saved them" (Judges 2:16). Samson was one of the judges whose task was to deliver the people from their enemies, the Philistines.

Before Samson was born, an angel appeared to Samson's once-barren mother to provide the lowdown on her future son. Samson and his mother were to take a Nazirite vow, a lifestyle of no haircuts, fermented drinks, or foods considered unclean (see Judges 13:6–14). The rest of the terms of this vow are described in Numbers 6:1–21.

Samson grew up blessed with strength above the norm. Alas, he also grew up willful and had a tendency to take his strength for granted, which led to trouble.

You know what happens when you meet the wrong person—the person who has a bad influence on your life. For Samson that person was Delilah, a woman from the Valley of Sorek. Having been paid by the Philistines to find out the source of Samson's strength, she put her feminine wiles to work.

Being of the mind-set that he could play with fire and not be burned, Samson told Delilah that he could be overcome by anyone who tied him with seven leather strips. So what did Delilah do? She bound him with seven leather strips—a trap Samson easily escaped. But instead of telling Delilah to hit the road after she tried to trap him the first time, Samson went along with yet another request for the source of his strength. "If anyone ties me securely with new ropes that have never been used, I'll become as weak as any other man," Samson declared (Judges 16:11). (And if you believe that, Delilah, there's some swamp property we're selling that you should buy as well!)

Delilah tried but failed to subdue Samson once again. Third time's the charm, right? Wrong. When weaving his hair into her loom didn't work, Delilah grew desperate and turned to nagging. Finally, Samson cracked under the pressure of her incessant nagging and told Delilah about his Nazirite vow. One haircut later, Samson found himself overpowered and blinded by the Philistines. The sad thing was that Samson didn't even realize that God no longer empowered him.

But God didn't forsake Samson. While the Philistines called for him to entertain them, Samson brought the house down by knocking down two pillars. Even in death, Samson was still allowed to be a conqueror, thanks to the grace of God.

This hair-raising incident with Samson is recorded in Judges 16.

The Urge to Usurp

Ishbosheth Bites Off More Than He Can Chew When He Tries to Become King of Israel

THROUGHOUT HISTORY and in the world of literature, there are stories of usurpers who schemed to gain thrones or dethrone rulers. William Shakespeare penned several plays on the subject. Who can forget Macbeth, the Scottish thane who schemed with his wife to murder the king and then stole the throne? Or how about Claudius, the scheming uncle of Hamlet, who murdered his own brother and became king of Denmark? And then there were the "friends" of Julius Caesar who plotted his assassination.

Ishbosheth wouldn't have placed himself in the category of usurper. After all, he was the son of Saul, the king of Israel—until Saul's death. Shouldn't a king's son expect to take the throne after the death of his father? Normally, yes. But back when Saul was king of Israel, he messed up royally by offering a sacrifice that the prophet Samuel was supposed to offer (see 1 Samuel 13). As a consequence, the prophet Samuel warned Saul that God planned to give the kingdom to another man—one outside the family of Saul. The chosen man was David, the son of Jesse. Samuel anointed David—the sign that he was God's chosen king (see 1 Samuel 16:1–13).

Yet even David refused to take the throne from Saul, preferring instead to wait until God declared that David's reign as king could begin. David continued to show respect for the man he deemed God's anointed, even after Saul's suicide.

While David was anointed king over Judah, Saul's loyal general, Abner, had Ishbosheth declared king over the rest of Israel. But when Ishbosheth later accused Abner of sleeping with Saul's concubine—an action that normally constituted a bid for the throne—Abner defected to David's side and angrily declared that David would be king over Israel (see 2 Samuel 3:6–11). With his main cheerleader gone, Ishbosheth worried about the shakiness of his position.

Abner's subsequent murder by Joab, David's loyal general, foreshadowed Ishbosheth's doom. Like Julius Caesar, Ishbosheth was eventually stabbed to death in his house by two war leaders who had easy access to him: Baanah and Recab. Expecting a reward from David, they found only death, however. An enraged David declared, "When wicked men have killed an innocent man in his own house and on his own bed—should I not now demand his blood from your hand and rid the earth of you!" (2 Samuel 4:11 NIV). David's men then killed Baanah and Recab.

In the book of Job, one of Job's friends stated, "I have observed, those who plow evil and those who sow trouble reap it" (Job 4:8 NIV). These words could serve as a warning for anyone with the urge to usurp.

Ishbosheth's story can be found in 2 Samuel 2:8–11 and 4:1–12.

Double Indemnity

For David, Double the Crime Means Double the Consequences

THERE'S AN OLD 1944 CLASSIC MOVIE titled *Double Indemnity,* which starred Fred MacMurray and Barbara Stanwyck and was based on a book by James M. Cain. In the movie, an insurance salesman and the woman with whom he was having an affair, schemed to murder her husband and gain the insurance money. They tried to perpetrate the perfect crime. While the film was considered shocking back in the day, imagine the way a similar true-life story was received. That story opened not on a movie screen, but on a rooftop in ancient Jerusalem.

Imagine you're the king of Israel—the top man in society, a man after God's own heart (see 1 Samuel 13:14). You've conquered enemies, won the hearts of beautiful women, and play a mean harp. In other words, you are the rock star of your day. So what are you going to do next, since Walt Disney World hadn't been built back then? For David, "next" involved lounging around the roof of his palace, bored out of his mind, instead of going to war with his army. "Next" meant falling into a heap of trouble.

Trouble came in the form of Bathsheba, the wife of Uriah the Hittite. Too bad David didn't make the same covenant that Job made: "I promised myself never to stare with desire at a young woman" (Job 31:1 CEV). For David, just one look was one look too many. One glimpse of Bathsheba's beauty, and David was hooked.

After sticking a toe in the waters of adultery, David soon discovered that Bathsheba was pregnant with his child.

What was a king to do, especially since David could not pawn off the pregnancy on Bathsheba's husband—his being away at war and all? David's plan for covering up his affair with Bathsheba involved murder and deceit (without the benefit of the insurance money). As king, he could order Uriah to the front lines during an attack, thus exponentially increasing Uriah's chances of being killed. He even ordered his general—Joab—to back the troops off to ensure Uriah's death.

Sadly, all went according to plan. Uriah was killed, thus freeing Bathsheba to marry David.

The perfect crime? Perhaps. But there was a major witness on the scene: God.

God dispatched the prophet Nathan to talk to David. Nathan spun a sad tale of a rich man who stole the lamb of a poor man—a story sure to provoke the king's sense of outrage and justice. But Nathan's epithet—"You are the man!" (2 Samuel 12:7 NIV)—was not a congratulatory verbal high five. Rather, it was a harsh indictment.

David was not described as a man after God's own heart for nothing. He immediately realized his sin and expressed his sorrow to the Lord. But the consequences of his sins were severe. Not only would the child Bathsheba give birth to die, but trouble would dog David's steps for the rest of his life. You have only to read the rest of 2 Samuel to find out the truth of that prophecy.

It just goes to show you—crime does pay; it pays double the consequences.

The story of David and Bathsheba is recorded in 2 Samuel 11–12.

Grapes of Wrath

Jezebel Schemes against Naboth and Reaps the Wrath of God

WHEN IT COMES to the evil kings and queens of Israel, Ahab and his wife Jezebel were in a league of their own. What abominations one didn't think of, the other was quick to come up with—a diabolical scheme of his or her own. Ahab and Jezebel set the bar when it came to downright dastardly deeds.

So when Ahab came home one evening in a foul mood, going to bed without dinner, Jezebel demanded, "What's going on here?" Turns out that Ahab had a bad case of sour grapes—his neighbor Naboth the Jezreelite's grapes, to be exact. Naboth had the unfortunate distinction of owning the vineyard next to Ahab's palace, which was the very spot that Ahab deemed as ideal. But when he approached Naboth about his plans to purchase his neighbor's vineyard, Naboth refused.

"Not on your life! So help me God, I'd never sell the family farm to you!" he told Ahab (1 Kings 21:3 MSG). He couldn't do it—this was family property and, by God's law, he needed to hold on to it for his family.

When Jezebel heard Ahab's sad saga, she gave her husband a verbal slap on the head, "Is this any way for a king of Israel to act? Aren't you the boss? On your feet! Eat! Cheer up! I'll take care of this; I'll get the vineyard of this Naboth the Jezreelite for you" (1 Kings 21:7). And Jezebel set to work doing what she did best—scheming and plotting.

First she sent out letters with Ahab's signature stamped on them to all the elders and civic leaders of Naboth's city, instructing them to call a fast day and to put Naboth at the head of the table. Jezebel further instructed them to strategically place two stool pigeons in front of Naboth who would jump up in the middle of the fast and say, "You! You blasphemed God and the king!" after which, the civic leaders would have no choice but to take Naboth out and stone him to death.

Now it may seem odd that anyone would actually follow such an overtly evil and propped-up scheme, but remember this was Jezebel and Ahab—not only the king and queen and absolute power in the land, but also the most evil couple to come along. So the elders and civic leaders did exactly as Jezebel instructed. Naboth was invited to the fast and was placed at the head of the table, and during the course of events, two lowlifes were brought in and accused Naboth of cursing the king and God. And just as Jezebel had plotted, Naboth was stoned to death.

As soon as Ahab heard the news, he ran over and claimed Naboth's vineyard as his own. Once again, Ahab and Jezebel seemingly prevailed and were victorious in getting what they wanted. But at the very moment that Ahab claimed the vineyard, God stepped in and told the prophet Elijah to confront Ahab.

The verdict? For his complicity in his wife's murderous plot and his theft of the vineyard, Ahab would not only suffer the consequences and be punished, but also all of his male descendants would be killed off. As God said, "I will most certainly bring doom upon you, make mincemeat of your descendants, kill off every sorry male wretch who's even remotely connected with the name Ahab" (1 Kings 21:21). Not good news for the family line.

It was worse for Jezebel. Because she was the mastermind of the plot, God reserved a special punishment for her: "Dogs will fight over the flesh of Jezebel all over Jezreel. Anyone tainted by

Ahab who dies in the city will be eaten by stray dogs; corpses in the country will be eaten by carrion crows" (1 Kings 21:23–24).

Grapes of wrath, indeed.

Read all about the battle for the vineyard in 1 Kings 21.

WOMEN LEADERS MENTIONED IN SCRIPTURE

WOMAN LEADER	WHERE	REFERENCE
Miriam	Protected little brother Moses as he floated in a basket on the Nile River; prophetess; acted in some ways as a leader but got in trouble when she complained about Moses' leadership	Exodus 2:4; 15:20; Numbers 12
Deborah	A prophetess and judge of Israel; along with Barak, was victorious over Sisera's army	Judges 4–5
Queen of Sheba	Also known as the Queen of the South; Sheba may have been located near southwestern Arabia; she had heard reports of the wisdom of Solomon, king of Israel, and traveled there to see for herself.	1 Kings 10:1–13; 2 Chronicles 9; Luke 11:31
Jezebel	Queen of the northern kingdom of Israel by marriage to King Ahab; daughter of King Ethbaal of the Sidonians; introduced Baal worship into the northern kingdom	1 Kings 16:31– 2 Kings 9:37

WOMAN LEADER	WHERE	REFERENCE
Athaliah	Mother of King Ahaziah of Judah; when her son died, she murdered the rest of the royal family in order to secure her place on the throne; one child was hidden from her and later presented as the true king.	2 Kings 11:1–16; 2 Chronicles 22:10–23:15
Huldah	Prophetess who gave God's message to King Josiah of Judah after God's law had been discovered in the temple	2 Kings 22:14–20
Esther	Jewish girl who married Xerxes, leader of the Medo-Persian empire; took her life in her hands to protect her people from extinction.	The book of Esther
Candace (Kandake)	Queen of Ethiopia; her treasurer met Philip on the road to Gaza and became a Christian.	Acts 8:27
Priscilla	Along with her husband, Aquila, served in ministry with Paul in Corinth; helped Apollos learn the full gospel message.	Acts 18; Romans 16:3–5; 1 Corinthians 16:19

Stonewalled

Tobiah and Sanballat Scheme against Nehemiah

A CITY WITHOUT WALLS in biblical times would be akin to a city today without a police force or any means of protecting its citizens. Defenseless, vulnerable, weak, exposed to its enemies. A city without walls was an object of scorn and ridicule.

Which was exactly the condition of Jerusalem when the Jewish exiles began returning home. The walls were in ruins. The city gates were cinders. The once majestic city, where God resided in his temple, had been reduced to rubble. When Nehemiah, the wine-taster for King Artaxerxes, heard of his beloved city's condition, he wept. Then he prayed. Then he took action.

With the king's blessing and God's guidance, Nehemiah returned to Jerusalem and began a massive reconstruction program. Under Nehemiah's direction, the people began to repair the city gates and rebuild the walls. Progress was quickly evident (read about that in "The Night Stalker," p. 51.)

In fact, the rebuilding was going so well that it caught the attention of Jerusalem's enemies—in particular, Sanballat and Tobiah. Furious to learn what was happening, Sanballat exploded, "What are these miserable Jews doing? Do they think they can get everything back to normal overnight? Make building stones out of make-believe?" (Nehemiah 4:2 MSG)

Undeterred by their enemies' ridicule, Nehemiah and the people kept on repairing and rebuilding the wall. Within a short time, the wall had been reconnected with no gaps and about half-way to its intended height.

When Sanballat and Tobiah heard that the project not only was continuing but was also going well, they decided to fight with more than words. The two plotted ways to cause as much trouble as possible. Nehemiah countered with prayer and a round-the-clock guard against their enemies, but the people became discouraged by the constant harassment. Soon the word around the city was that the workers were pooped, unable to finish the task.

Sanballat and Tobiah were elated. They escalated their efforts and began using fear tactics, "They won't know what hit them. Before they know it we'll be at their throats, killing them right and left. *That* will put a stop to the work!" (Nehemiah 4:11) Soon the workers began sounding the alarm—at least ten times a day: "We're surrounded! We're going to be attacked!"

Nehemiah realized that work couldn't continue under such conditions. So he stationed guards at the most vulnerable places in the wall. He assigned people by families with swords, lances, and bows. Half the men worked, while the other half stood guard. Workers had a tool in one hand and a spear in the other. And Nehemiah took the added precaution of having a trumpeter at his side to sound the alarm in case of an attack.

Work resumed, but Sanballat and Tobiah were not about to quit. Next, they tried to intimidate Nehemiah by telling him everyone knew that he was rebuilding the wall so he could be king—and that they were going to tell King Artaxerxes. When that didn't work, they sent a "prophet" to Nehemiah with a warning to meet at God's temple and find safety "because they're coming to kill you." Once again, Nehemiah countered with prayer: "O my God, don't let Tobiah and Sanballat get by with all the mischief they've done" (Nehemiah 6:14).

Despite the constant opposition and plotting, Nehemiah and the people completed the job in a record fifty-two days. The people rejoiced while their enemies returned home, demoralized and humiliated.

But the restored walls stood as a testimony to what can be accomplished when God's people join together to solve a problem with God's help. The final outcome was never in doubt.

The sinister scheme to keep Jerusalem's walls from being rebuilt is found in Nehemiah 4 and 6.

Haman's Inhumanity

Haman Plots the Destruction of the Jews

TALK ABOUT DRAMA. Esther's story contains enough nail-biting drama to keep you on the edge of your seat.

The story unfolds during the time of Israel's exile. Conquering the Babylonians, the Medes and Persians rose to power. We first meet Esther in a Cinderella moment—she wins a beauty contest and becomes the new queen, the wife of Xerxes, king of Persia. Although Esther was Jewish, she kept that fact from Xerxes, having been advised by her cousin Mordecai to hide her heritage.

As is the case with many great stories, the life of a courageous heroine is often juxtaposed with that of an antagonist. And Haman is perfectly hiss-worthy in the role of villain. Just about the time that Esther became queen, Haman also received a promotion in

Xerxes's government. Haman enjoyed the fact that all of the royal officials paid him homage—everyone except Mordecai, who refused to bow as Haman passed. For this perceived insult, Haman decided that all of the Jews—Mordecai's people—had to die. Talk about overkill!

Haman's first step in his scheme was to spin a lie about the Jews' civil disobedience, in the hopes of tricking the king into making a law giving Persians the authority to kill any and every Jewish person in the kingdom. According to Persian law, once a law was written on the books and sealed with the king's seal, it could not be changed.

The king agreed with Haman's plan. Now Haman had only to sit back and wait for the death order to be carried out.

Now this is the part of most dramas where the heroine is alerted to the villain's evil scheme and decides to take action. The story of Esther does not disappoint. Mordecai discovered the new law, and after weeping and fasting, he told Esther about it. Now was the time for her to go before the king and beg him for the lives of their people.

In Esther's life, no music swelled—the cue for high drama in movies. This was real life. Only the pounding of her heart signaled the fact that she was the key player in a life-or-death matter. If she went before the king without being first summoned she could be put to death. But if she didn't go before the king, her people would all die. As Mordecai so eloquently put it,

> Do not think that because you are in the king's house you alone of all the Jews will escape. For if you remain silent at this time, relief and deliverance for the Jews will arise from another place, but you and your father's family will perish. And who knows but that you have come to royal position for such a time as this? (Esther 4:13–14 NIV)

Esther made the decision not to save herself, but to save others. After fasting, she went before the king. Fortunately, he gladly received her. But instead of pleading her case there and then, she decided to bide her time and invite the king and Haman to a banquet.

Why would Esther draw out the tension by throwing a dinner party? Her delay was undoubtedly part of God's plan. Although he isn't mentioned directly in the book of Esther, you can see God's actions behind the scenes.

Before the banquet took place, Haman really showed his inhumanity. He planned a special death for Mordecai—custom-building a gallows just for him. His rage at Mordecai's lack of respect continually spurred Haman's spite.

Alas for Haman, the king had a sleepless night and decided he would read some of the chronicles of his reign. As he read, he discovered that Mordecai had at one time saved his life by uncovering an assassination plot. He decided to honor Mordecai, which, of course, steamed Haman.

But the worst was yet to come. During Esther's banquet, the plot to kill the Jews became interesting dinner conversation. As Esther pleaded for the lives of the Jews—her people—Haman's terror grew. But as he tried to plead for *his* life, the king misinterpreted his actions as an attack against the queen.

You've heard of poetic justice—the concept that good deeds are rewarded while evil deeds are punished in a fitting way. Well . . . Haman wound up hanged on the very gallows he had built for Mordecai. As for Esther, she saved her people, thanks to a new decree the king dictated (see Esther 8–9).

God often specializes in nick-of-time rescues. He delights in placing just the right people in just the right place . . . for such a time as this.

Read this compelling story in Esther 3–7.

Wild Things

The King's Envious Advisers Scheme against Daniel and End Up with the Lions

BEING EATEN by a wild creature is one of the most horrific images we can imagine. So what kind of sinister mind comes up with a plan to have a person fed to lions?

Daniel 6 relates a story of professional jealousy gone wild. The king of the Medes and Persians established a council of several dozen regional governors (satraps) from the vast territories his alliance had recently conquered. For efficiency's sake, he had them report to three presidents. One of those three principal officials was Daniel. He had so distinguished himself above the others that King Darius wanted to make him the prime minister, the man in charge. The other satraps, meanwhile, were struck with jealousy and tried to wreck his nomination.

But they could find nothing in his record—no corruption, no sex scandal, no mishandling of funds—nothing that would implicate him in some typical political scandal and slow the process of appointment.

"You know, there is *one* thing he's rather obsessive about," someone ventured. "Have you noticed that this guy never stops praying to his hometown god back in Jerusalem? I mean, it's kinda silly. He was dragged away from there sixty years ago by the Babylonians when he was just a lad, and he's lived here in Babylon ever since, but he's never given up the habit of praying to their national god. You can see him there in his window every afternoon, facing Jerusalem, and praying to him."

A current of electricity circulated throughout the assembly as one by one they recognized the truth of this assessment. "We've got him!" they told each other confidently. And sure enough, it didn't take much persuasion to butter up the old king and get him to see the "wisdom" in declaring an official proclamation: for one month, no one could address any prayers of petition to anyone else but to Darius the king. Yes sir, to no other king, no other god, nobody. Anybody found in violation of the edict would be thrown into the den of lions, a sort of zoo near the palace. "This will make it plain to all throughout the empire that there is only one authority, and it's you, O king," the advisers said. Flattered, the king signed the proclamation.

Jubilant, the conspirators went to wait outside Daniel's window. Would he comply with the king's decree, or would he continue his lifelong habit of praying to the God of Israel? They didn't have to wait long, and they weren't disappointed. When Daniel appeared in the window and knelt down on his knees facing Jerusalem as he always did, they knew they had him. They raced back to the palace with the accusation and demanded that Daniel be thrown into the lions' pit. The king tried every way he could to absolve Daniel of the penalty, but the bureaucrats pressed upon him that his proclamation could not possibly be annulled: it was a "law of the Medes and the Persians, which cannot be revoked" (Daniel 6:8 ESV).

Reluctantly, the king eventually submitted to his underlings. With great glee they watched as Daniel was thrown into the pit. As they closed the door over Daniel, the king called out a last word of encouragement: "May your God, whom you serve continually, deliver you!" (Daniel 6:16).

The king couldn't eat or sleep the whole night through, so sick was he from the injustice and the senselessness of this petty vengeance on the part of his selected administrators. As soon as it started to get light, he ran to the lions' pit and called out plaintively to Daniel, hoping he might somehow have survived. Daniel answered cheerfully, "We're fine, King Darius. The angels shut the lions' mouths so they couldn't touch me. You know, come to think of it, they do look extra hungry. You better not come too close to the entrance . . ."

"That's all right," said the king, "I've got a fine breakfast for them. Bring those men who accused Daniel and throw *them* into this pit. While you're at it, bring the rest of their families too. These beasts do indeed look like they're hungry."

They were, apparently. The Bible says that when all the "bad guys" were thrown into the pit, the lions tore them to pieces before their feet even reached the ground.

To read more about this story, see Daniel 6.

Herod on the Hunt

Herod Schemes to Use the Magi to Get to Baby Jesus

ONE OF THE most cold-blooded killers in all history carried the self-appointed title "King of the Jews." For Herod the Great, son of Antipater the Idumean (or Edomite), the turbulent times in which Julius Caesar rose to power in the Roman empire fifty years before Christ were also an opportunity for adventurers like himself to rise in power and influence in the land we call Israel or Palestine. He ingratiated himself to three Roman emperors in succession—

Julius, then Antony, then Antony's rival Octavian, who later became known as Caesar Augustus.

But enjoying Roman sanction of his quest to be "King of the Jews" did not put the rule in his back pocket. Far from it. In Palestine, the Hasmonean dynasty (a dwindling faction left over from the heady days of the Maccabees a century before) despised his Edomite bloodline. And the priesthood at Jerusalem was aghast at his willingness to accommodate Roman emperors' claims of deity and to build pagan temples, theaters, and sports arenas throughout the land. Many times Herod cut short frustrating negotiations by having those who opposed him murdered.

He also suffered from paranoia. The slightest rumor of betrayal or disloyalty would set him off on a bloody purge of the feared conspirators. Once he killed an uncle; another time his father-in-law. He even killed his own wife, whom he loved very much, when she was accused of disloyalty. A Roman emperor joked, "I'd rather be Herod's pig than be his son," an allusion to the Jewish law of not eating pork and to Herod's having two of his sons killed whom he thought to be conspiring for his throne.

By the time he reached a disease-ridden old age, his crimes weighed heavily on his conscience, but he would not give up his evil machinations. He knew that his imminent death would be the cause of rejoicing in the streets of Jerusalem, and he hated that thought. So to prevent that, he gave orders to execute a long list of his political enemies among the Jewish families when he died, so that the only sound one would hear after his death was that of mourning. What an incredibly evil man!

Thus, his sole appearance in the Bible (which takes place in those last months of his long life) perfectly accords with the historical figure we know as Herod the Great. The horrible story of the massacre of the infants around Bethlehem sounds like a dark fairy tale, an ogre story made up by some perturbed imagination. Unfortunately, however, it resonates in perfect pitch with what we know of Herod from well-documented secular history.

After a lifetime of scrapping for power, having invested millions in the Jerusalem temple to placate that wing of his lukewarm supporters, and having killed dozens of rivals, Herod was livid at the news circulating in the streets of Jerusalem that some Chaldean astrologers (Magi, or wise men) had come looking for "the child born to be king of the Jews" (Matthew 2:2 CEV). He called in these wise men and also some Jewish scholars, trying to get as much information as he could. When he had pretty much narrowed down the location of the infant the wise men were seeking, he asked them to come back and inform him of the child's whereabouts once they'd found him. "Er, umm . . . so that I *too* may come and worship him!" he added, with a sickly pious smile before sending them on their way. Makes you shudder, doesn't it?

When an angelic warning to the wise men thwarted the old king's plot, and when the king realized that they went home without reporting to him, his rage overflowed. He sent soldiers to kill every male infant in Bethlehem who might be even close to the age of the newborn king.

Christian art from most cultures to which the gospel has gone portrays this part of the Christmas story more often than you would expect. There's something about the plot and tone of the story—an evil, murderous tyrant, innocent women and children as victims, narrowly escaped danger for the infant protagonist—that gives us hope. It shows that even in a world where nasty ogres rule, a sovereign God rules providentially above them.

For more about Herod and the wise men, read Matthew 2.

WHAT'S WITH ALL THE HERODS?

The Bible lists several Herods, and the following chart will help keep them straight.

WHICH HEROD	REFERENCE	WHAT HE'S KNOWN FOR
Herod the Great	Matthew 2:1–18	Rebuilt the temple in Jerusalem, killed the infant males in Bethlehem
Herod Archelaus, oldest son of Herod the Great	Matthew 2:22	He was the king when Joseph and Mary returned with Jesus from Egypt.
Herod Philip, son of Herod the Great	Matthew 14:3	He was the first husband of Herodias, who left him to marry Antipas, his brother.
Herod Antipas, youngest son of Herod the Great	Matthew 14:1–12; Mark 6:14–29; Luke 9:7–9; 23:6–12	Killed John the Baptist; interrogated and mocked Jesus before sending him back to Pilate
Herod Agrippa I, grandson of Herod the Great	Acts 12:1–4, 20–23	Executed James and imprisoned Peter; died "eaten by worms" (V.23)
Herod Agrippa II, great-grandson of Herod the Great	Acts 25:13–26:32	Interrogated Paul before sending him to Rome

The Kiss of Death

Judas Agrees to Betray Jesus with a Kiss

"ET TU, BRUTE?" From Shakespeare's *Julius Caesar*, this is one of the most well-known statements of betrayal ever spoken—the sad acknowledgment by Julius Caesar of his friend Marcus Junias Brutus's betrayal. But the name most associated with betrayal is *Judas*. And it all started with thirty pieces of silver.

The Pharisees and other Jewish leaders decided that Jesus, the popular teacher and healer, had to go. They couldn't stand his sermons, his habit of healing on the Sabbath, and most of all, the way he challenged their authority. But how could they get rid of him? He continually slipped out of their many traps of rhetoric.

Judas, one of Jesus' disciples, gave them just the opportunity they needed. He went to the chief priests to volunteer to betray Jesus. It is said that every man has his price, and for Judas, the price was thirty pieces of silver—about a year's salary. Now the onus was on Judas to find the perfect time and the perfect place to do the deed. The signal would be a kiss. He chose the Passover feast as the perfect time.

Jesus seemed unusually grave during the Passover meal, knowing that the time of his suffering had drawn near. But the worst of it was that he was going to be betrayed by one of his chosen disciples.

He took a piece of bread and dipped it, knowing that the person he handed it to was the betrayer. This was one of the men whose feet he washed that night. As he handed the bread to Judas, Scripture tells us, "Right then Satan took control of Judas" (John 13:27

CEV). Jesus didn't try to talk him out of what he was about to do. Judas's resolve was already hardened.

When Jesus decided to go to the Garden of Gethsemane to pray, only eleven of his disciples went with him. But the twelfth disciple met him in the midst of a crowd—a crowd of soldiers and Jewish officials armed to the teeth with swords.

This was the perfect place. Judas stepped forward to greet Jesus with a kiss. Imagine the bitter tang of that normally loving act. "Et tu, Judas?" Jesus could have said, but he refrained from blame. He was about to suffer a death made possible by the betrayal of a friend. But he knew it was all in his Father's plan.

To read more about Judas's betrayal, read Matthew 26:14–25, 47–56. (See also Mark 14:1–2, 10–11, 43–50; Luke 22:1–6, 47–53; and John 18:1–9.)

The Vow

A Group of Jews Scheme to Kill Paul

PAUL HAD A WAY of bringing out the best and the worst in people. He wasn't the kind of orator who made people stroke their beards thoughtfully and say, "Hmmmm." With Paul, a person either bought what he said full strength and it turned his life upside down forever after, or a person rejected his message with a ferocious snarl.

On his last visit to Jerusalem, Paul stirred up the animosity of

the latter kind of people. Some of these Jews had argued with him
for years, losing most of the debates, and they were tired of it. They
remained unconvinced of Paul's claims about Jesus' being the Messiah and the Son of God. They decided enough was enough.

Forty bitterly determined men took a solemn vow that they
would neither eat nor drink until they had killed Paul. Their pro-
posal to the Jewish council of religious leaders (also called the San-
hedrin) that they cooperate in getting rid of this troublemaker was
met with enthusiasm. Here's how it would go down, they agreed:
The Jewish council would ask the Roman centurion guarding Paul
to bring him down to their meeting room so they could question
him further. When the soldiers brought Paul out of his protective
custody in the Roman military quarters and led him toward the
Jewish enclave, the assassins would fall upon him and stab him to
death. Their force of forty should be sufficient to overcome the
handful of soldiers that would be accompanying Paul. A few bloody
strokes and he'd be through, and they'd be done with him.

It probably would have worked except for the tiny little fact that
the plot was overheard by, of all people, Paul's own nephew, who
was somewhere nearby listening. That young man ran to the Roman
garrison and reported the plot to the tribune in charge of the whole
company of Roman soldiers. The tribune saw an opportunity to re-
cover his loss of face suffered the day before. He had come within a
whisker of publicly scourging Paul, whom he did not know was a
Roman citizen. When he learned his error, he was most conciliatory
and sought a way to ingratiate himself. This was the looked-for opportunity.

The tribune ordered a detachment of seventy horsemen, two
hundred soldiers, and two hundred more spearmen—a formidable
force—to be sent along with Paul to Caesarea, the Roman capital
down the highway to the sea. He also sent along a self-promoting
letter to the Roman governor that put a favorable spin on his own
intervention in the conflict between Paul and the Jews, making it
appear that he had originally "rescued" Paul from the hands of the

Jews because he was a Roman citizen. Now he was completing the rescue, he wrote, sending Paul away from the rising danger to where he'd be safe from the conspiracy.

We have to wonder what happened to all those hungry would-be killers the next morning when they learned that the object of their vow had absconded in the night, surrounded by a nearly impregnable force of Roman spears and swords. Did they renounce their vows in a loud lament of grief and anger? Or did they only eventually give up on the plan, one by one, and slip away for some nice bread and lentils?

To read more about this incident, see Acts 23:12–35.

PART FOUR

Exceptional Escapes

Flood Insurance

Noah and His Family Travel in an Ark to Escape the Flood

WHEN WE THINK of the Noah story, we inevitably think of animals. What a picture we conjure up. All those animals paired off like wedding couples coming to the ark, docile as farm creatures, with a cacophony of quacking, hooting, snuffling, trumpeting, roaring, squeaking, and chirping. All those cute little animals remind us of a fun day at the zoo.

But we miss the real point of the story when we sentimentalize it this way. When Jesus referred back to this story, it was as a warning about the implacable swiftness of the judgment of God. Jesus warned his listeners that the coming of the Son of Man in judgment would be an unwelcome, terrifying surprise for many unprepared people (see Matthew 24:37–39 and Luke 17:26–27).

Indeed, when Genesis pulls back the curtain on God's thoughts before he sent the Flood, it is a terrifying scenario:

> GOD saw that human evil was out of control. People thought evil, imagined evil—evil, evil, evil from morning to night. GOD was sorry that he had made the human race in the first place; it broke his heart. GOD said, "I'll get rid of my ruined creation, make a clean sweep: people, animals, snakes and bugs, birds—the works. I'm sorry I made them."(Genesis 6:5–7 MSG)

That was the context—God's unmitigated fury poured out to scour and remove the human race from the face of the earth.

Then, this short caveat appears: "But Noah was different. God liked what he saw in Noah" (Genesis 6:8). We are told that Noah "walked with God" (Genesis 6:9 NIV). Noah had the ultimate flood insurance: faith and obedience.

No one should read this story too glibly. It looked for a while that God actually was going to destroy all of creation—and he came close to doing that. That God provided a means of escape for Noah and his family and a mated pair of every species of creature on earth is a great blessing. It demonstrates God's great mercy; he did save enough human beings to start the project over again.

To grasp just how great the miracle of that salvation is, we have to first stop and recognize how great is the destruction from which they were saved. The image of that ark floating for ten months on the surface of a deluged and silent planet should be etched into our too-quickly restless imaginations. Sin was punished with death.

Noah and his family weren't perfect, but they had faith in God, and that was enough. And God made the promise, with a rainbow in the clouds, that he wouldn't destroy the earth with a flood again.

Remember the ark, remember the rainbow, and remember the mercy of God.

To read more about Noah and the Flood, read Genesis 6–9.

Assaulted at Sodom

Lot Escapes the Conflagration at Sodom and Gomorrah

AFTER READING about school shootings and terrorist activities, many people say that the world couldn't get any worse. How could anything be worse than when the innocent are harmed and justice is denied? Nothing *could* be worse. As we look at the newspaper or check out Internet news sources, we realize the world still continues despite the evil actions of its inhabitants. But there was a time when even God said, "Enough is enough!" and decided to put an end to two cities where evil had become an everyday matter.

Dateline: Sodom and Gomorrah. Two cities in the Jordan Valley blessed with a nearby water source. Who wouldn't want to live there? If you read "Lot's Family Values" (p. 28), you know that Lot, Abraham's nephew, couldn't resist moving to Sodom.

But as beautiful as the area was, the wrongs done there made it extremely ugly to God. In fact, he sent two angels to let Abraham know that the end was near for Sodom and Gomorrah. Read Genesis 18 to see how Abraham bargained with God in order to save Sodom and thus save his nephew's family too. God listened to Abraham, but ultimately, the two angels still were directed toward Sodom.

Lot met the angels at the gate. Whether or not he knew they were angels, the Bible does not say. Since they had bodies, perhaps he believed they were important travelers in the area. Being a man governed by the customs of hospitality, as was his uncle Abraham, Lot invited the two men home. Surprisingly, they refused to go with him at first. They couldn't help noticing Lot's desperation as he begged them to *please* follow him to his home. So they went.

A lovely evening was soon irrevocably ruined by the arrival of the men of the town. These unexpected guests were not so unexpected, judging by Lot's earlier insistence that the angels return with him to the safety of his home. The mob of men had one request: send out your guests and allow us to have our way with them! (Hence, the introduction of *sodomy* to the lexicon.)

Lot, being the loving father that he was, had a better idea. He would send out his unmarried daughters instead. In that way, he wouldn't violate the laws of hospitality. Well, this was a bargain the men of the town refused. Their ultimatum was this: send out the two guys, or else suffer the consequences.

The angels chose the "or else" option but came up with their own consequences. Every man outside of Lot's home was hit with instant blindness, courtesy of the angels.

Playtime was over. The destruction of Sodom and Gomorrah was imminent. The angels could have used today's oft-quoted line, "Come with me if you want to live," as they talked with Lot and his family. Dawn was the deadline.

Lot's almost-sons-in-law refused to flee. And even Lot dawdled about leaving with just the clothes on his back. Since the angels could not destroy the city with Lot still in it, they practically pushed Lot and his family out of town, with the strong warning to avoid looking back. Their warning was not a metaphor to forget the past and move on. Physically turning and looking back would have serious consequences.

Lot, his wife, and their daughters had to run for their lives. Their destination, according to the strong suggestion of the angels, was the mountains. But Lot didn't think he could make it and begged to be allowed to go only as far as the next town—Zoar.

As soon as they were clear of the cities, God let loose. The once beautiful plain was soon an ash heap. Lot's wife made the mistake of looking back. It was the last mistake she would ever make. Instantly, she was turned into a pillar of salt. But the rest of Lot's family was saved. God honored Abraham's request.

Read more about Lot and the angels in Genesis 19:1–29.

River Rescue

Moses Is Rescued from the River

GOSHEN WAS THE LAND where Joseph's relatives settled in Egypt. This lush green delta was formed when the Nile River gently dropped the rich silt it picked up for a thousand miles along the way. Jacob and his wagon train of seventy progeny spread out in this benign, fertile territory. The band of seventy merrily grew to thousands, then thousands of thousands, until the native Egyptians became alarmed.

"We've got to stop these accursed Hebrews from continuing to procreate so prolifically," proclaimed the Pharaoh. "Tell the mid-wives to kill male babies the moment they come out of the womb, before the mother even knows what's happened! She'll think the child was born dead." But that didn't work. The Hebrew midwives feared God more that they feared Pharaoh, so they made up stories to cover the facts that they let Hebrew boy babies live. God blessed the midwives for their piety by giving *them* families of their own! The Hebrews continued to multiply like rabbits.

Frustrated, the Egyptian king made a more drastic declaration: "If a Hebrew baby boy is born, throw him into the Nile River!"

One Hebrew mother was so taken with the handsome features of her newborn son that she kept him hidden. It was easy enough to do for a while. But after three months, the boy's voice had developed, and he could cry full throttle and be heard at a distance. The Israelites had long lived in the swampy delta country of Goshen, and the mother was familiar with the reedy papyrus plants that grew everywhere. She took some and wove them into a basket, covered it with tar and pitch to waterproof it, and then tucked her baby carefully into this floating cradle.

With her daughter promising to stay and watch, the woman placed the little raft upon the shallow waters among the reeds that crowded together along the banks of the Nile. She thus fulfilled the letter of the law; in case anyone saw her and asked, she had indeed put her son in the Nile River! The sister of the baby in the papyrus basket stood just far enough away to be disassociated in the eyes of anyone who happened along, but close enough to come running if needed.

Then the story takes an enormous twist, becoming one of the greatest ironies of all time. Who should appear next on the scene but the daughter of Pharaoh, the very man who was trying to kill all these male Hebrew babies! But when she opened the basket and saw the face of the dear child, she was totally overwhelmed with pity. "The poor sweet thing! He's hungry. What can we give this baby to eat?"

The boy's sister saw that as her cue to intervene. "Would you like me to try to find someone from among the Hebrew women who live nearby, someone who could nurse the child for you?"

"Oh, that would be perfect! Will you, please?" The Egyptian princess readily assented to the practical wisdom of the suggestion. So the girl ran off to get . . . her own mother, naturally. Mom was *paid* to nurse her own child until he was old enough to live in the king's palace as his adopted grandson.

Eventually the boy entered the king's palace and grew up in privileged conditions. The princess named him *Moses.* "I drew him out of the water" (Exodus 2:10 NIV). Little did she know that her river-rescued son would be the one to defeat Pharaoh and deliver all Israel out of his hand. What delicious irony!

To read more about the story of Moses' birth, see Exodus 2:1–10.

Did You See the Sea?

The Hebrews Are Caught between the Red Sea and Pharaoh's Pursuing Army

MOST OF US have seen the movie. You know, the famous scene in *The Ten Commandments,* where Moses (actor Charlton Heston) holds out his hand over the sea, and the water spectacularly divides, permitting the Israelites to flee across on temporarily dry soil.

Movies are fine, but it's well worth the time to go back and read the original story. Those poor Hebrew slaves had never been more than a mile from home. After God's deliverance from Pharaoh, they covered a lot of strange territory in one day, leaving the familiar haunts of Egypt farther and farther behind. There must have been some Israelites who realized they were free at last and began to celebrate and kick up their heels.

All of them, though, were brought back to sober reality when a rumor spread rapidly from the farthest ranks at the back: "We hear a clanking of iron and see a cloud of dust . . . the Egyptians are coming after us! Pharaoh sent his army out after we left, and they're roaring toward us and will overtake us in about an hour!"

Then an even worse piece of news bounced from the front ranks to the back: "Well, we've reached the banks of a body of water, a veritable sea. There's no way across, and it's too wide to go around." Stuck between the sea and Pharaoh's army! By sunset, Pharaoh's army had indeed caught up with the vast hoard of Israelites and other refugees from Egypt who were all milling around on the banks of the Red Sea, wondering what in the world they were going to do. They were, for all intents and purposes, trapped.

The strange thing that happened next, however, was nothing less than a miracle. Like a man might pick up a lantern and move it, God moved the bright cloud of his presence directly between the camp of Israel and the advancing Egyptians. As darkness settled over the desert, the cloud stood brightly burning, like a sort of curtain between the two huge groups of adversaries. God made the cloud absorb and extinguish all light on the Egyptian side of this curtain, so that it was pitch black in the Egyptian army camp all night long—they couldn't see a thing. He reflected so much light out onto the Israelite camp that they, in turn, moved around almost as in daylight.

At dawn, God said "Move out!" and they did, crossing over right through the middle of the sea, now a dry seabed. When they'd all safely arrived on the other side, they looked back to see the Egyptians following them again. Bad mistake. Suddenly, halfway across the eerie water-walled canyon, their chariot wheels started veering left and right, chaos broke out, and the walls collapsed. Two halves of a sea collided together with a thunderous splashy clap. Not an Egyptian was to be seen again, except as the roiling waters occasionally rolled a body up from the depths.

And that was that.

To read more about this miraculous escape, see Exodus 13–14.

Michal Makes a Way

Michal Risks Her Father's Wrath to Help David Escape

WHO IS MICHAL? Let's start with a better understanding of who David was. Besides being the son of Jesse, he was a shepherd boy, the anointed king-to-be (see 1 Samuel 16), and a giant killer (see 1 Samuel 17). He also was a musician skilled enough to be hired by Saul, the king of Israel. Some people have lives with lots of gusto.

Saul gave his daughter, Michal, to David as a reward for killing about two hundred Philistines—the enemies of Israel (see 1 Samuel 18). The bride price had been the lives of one hundred Philistines, but David was an overachiever.

Michal was fine with the plan. After all, the words *handsome* and *heroic* were part of her vocabulary. And David was both. Plus, she was in love with David.

Being the jealous type, Saul had big plans for his son-in-law, plans that involved killing him as soon as possible. Saul greatly resented David's popularity, particularly the folk song made up comparing Saul to David: "Saul has struck down his thousands, and David his ten thousands" (1 Samuel 18:7 ESV). It had a catchy beat, but Saul refused to dance to it. Also, he refused to give up the throne and become king emeritus. He wouldn't have to do that if David died first.

Saul tried to enlist the help of family, namely his son Jonathan. But Jonathan stubbornly refused to participate in the killing of his best friend. There was only one thing left to do—send in the assassins. By morning, the world would be Davidless.

Having learned of the plot, Michal quickly told her husband, "You have to run for it or you'll die!" The window was the only way. She quickly lowered him down to the street. To fool her father's assassins, she placed a small household idol in the bed and covered it with goat's hair.

By the time they arrived, David was long gone.

Saul was furious with Michal's "David's in bed sick" story. But Michal was ready with yet another piece of fiction: David had threatened to kill her if she didn't help him escape.

People do the craziest things when they're in love.

Michal makes a way of escape in 1 Samuel 19:11–17.

Crazy Like a Fox

David Fakes Insanity to Escape from King Achish

DESPERATION OR DESPAIR can drive people to do what they wouldn't normally do. Desperation was a state that David lived in for several years. It finally drove him off the edge of sanity—or so it seemed.

Modern dramas with their knife-edge suspense and amazing getaways have nothing on the life of David. Imagine having the most powerful man in the land adding your death to his daily to-do list. Welcome to David's world.

Fed up with David's fame among his subjects, Israel's king

Saul declared war not just with the Philistines—the real enemies of Israel—but with David. So David, the original public enemy number one, was on the run for many years. He gained help from his best friend, Jonathan, who disagreed with his father's assessment of David (see 1 Samuel 19). But even Jonathan couldn't dissuade Saul from his hatred of David. And with the APB out on David, it was only a matter of time before Saul or his men caught up with him.

The law of Moses established cities of refuge where accused murderers (involuntary manslaughter) could go to avoid being killed by vengeful friends and relatives (see Numbers 35:6–28). But Saul's determination to kill David made even those cities unsafe for him to dwell in. There was only one choice left—to head to the cities of the Philistines. This was a place where no sane Israelite man would venture.

Gath was the city of choice for David. If the name sounds familiar, think back to Goliath—the giant David killed. Gath was Goliath's hometown.

Achish, the king, had heard of David's fame. The folk song, "Saul has struck down his thousands, and David his ten thousands" (1 Samuel 21:11 ESV) was a top-forty hit playing on Gath's airwaves. Instead of being flattered, David was afraid. Perhaps he feared that the people of Gath would find some reason to kill him too. After all, their hometown hero, Goliath, had been killed by David. Faking insanity was the only sane thing to do!

David went the whole nine yards: drooling, marking on walls. He had to be convincing, so that Achish would not view him without disgust. But the best part about it was that Achish could not view him as a threat. David soon escaped from Gath.

He was crazy all right. Crazy like a fox.

To read more about David's insane adventure, read 1 Samuel 21:10–15.

The Great Escape

David Plays "Catch Me If You Can" with Saul

J ASON BOURNE slips out of sight and away from the CIA agents during a suspense-filled chase through a busy railway terminal in *The Bourne Ultimatum*. Trinity leaps off a roof and through a window to escape the agents in *The Matrix*. Mary Jane Watson barely escapes being crushed by a car in a huge spider web in *Spider-Man 3*. These are the kinds of great escapes we're used to—the cinematic kind, complete with popcorn. But some of the greatest escapes have occurred in real life.

David, the shepherd boy turned man on the run, didn't start off life as an escape artist. As Shakespeare wrote in *Twelfth Night*, "Some are born great, some achieve greatness and some have greatness thrust upon them." David had greatness thrust upon him by being anointed the king of Israel (see 1 Samuel 16). Unfortunately, this was a job Saul already had. Not content to give up the throne, a not-in-his-right-mind Saul decided to kill David. Thus began David's life on the run.

The tension mounted as Saul learned of David's latest hiding place near En Gedi. At last his quarry was within his grasp. Taking three thousand men, he hurried to the cave where David and his traveling companions were said to be hiding. Little did Saul know that the tables were just about to be turned. Instead of finding David, David found Saul in a vulnerable position.

David's men assured David that this was the moment for revenge. He could kill Saul and be free of worry. The men tried to justify killing Saul by mentioning God: "The LORD told you he was going to let you defeat your enemies and do whatever you want with them. This must be the day the LORD was talking about" (1 Samuel 24:4 CEV).

But David refused to kill Saul. Instead, he cut off a piece of Saul's robe without Saul's noticing—an amazing feat.

When Saul left the cave, David called to him, holding up the piece of Saul's robe. He told Saul, "Look at what I'm holding. You can see that it's a piece of your robe. If I could cut off a piece of your robe, I could have killed you. But I let you live, and that should prove I'm not trying to harm you" (1 Samuel 24:11).

If you were Saul, how would you feel, confronted by the enemy you wanted to kill, but who could have killed you at any moment? Saul instantly felt ashamed of his actions and realized that this time the great escape was not David's but his.

Read about the great escape of Saul and David in 1 Samuel 24.

DAVID'S RUN-INS WITH SAUL

David and Saul had a volatile relationship. Saul's many attempts to murder David had something to do with it.

THE RUN-IN	THE RESULT
While David played soothing music for Saul in Saul's home, Saul threw a spear at him.	The spear missed David (1 Samuel 19:9–10).
Saul sent assassins to kill David at his home.	David's wife Michal helped him escape out of a window (1 Samuel 19:11–17).
David tried to escape Saul by fleeing to the home of Samuel the prophet in Ramah.	Saul sent three groups of men to pursue David at Ramah. But the Spirit of God caused each group to prophesy. When Saul went to Ramah, he also prophesied, thus enabling David to escape (1 Samuel 19:18–24).

THE RUN-IN	THE RESULT
After Saul threw a spear at him, a disbelieving Jonathan discovered the truth of his father's murderous vendetta against David.	Jonathan warned David to escape (1 Samuel 20).
David headed first to Nob, then to Gath to escape from Saul.	David pretended to be insane out of fear of Achish, the king of Gath (1 Samuel 21).
David escaped from Gath and headed to the cave at Adullam. There he became the leader of a band of men.	Saul pursued David and wound up killing the priests at Nob (1 Samuel 22).
After David was told of the slaughter of priests, he went to Keilah to fight against the Philistines.	Saul planned to trap David and his men in Keilah. When David heard from God that Saul planned to force the people to surrender him, David escaped to Horesh in the Desert of Ziph (1 Samuel 23:1–18).
The Ziphites betrayed David to Saul.	David and his men escaped down one side of a mountain while Saul and his men searched another. Saul only broke off the pursuit when told that the Philistines were about to raid (1 Samuel 23:19–29).
David escaped to En Gedi.	In a cave, David had an opportunity to kill Saul but did not (1 Samuel 24).
The Ziphites again betrayed David to Saul, explaining that David hid on a hill of Hakilah.	Saul sent an army after David. While the Lord caused Saul and his men to fall asleep, David went down to Saul's camp and took Saul's spear and water jug, instead of killing him as Abishai suggested. David then escaped to Philistine territory. Saul finally stopped searching for David (1 Samuel 26–27:4).

A Good King
Cleans House

Hezekiah Stands Strong in the Face of Great Opposition

MOST OF THE KINGS who sat on David's throne after him were measured and found wanting. In the long, grim list of failures, king after king was described in this way: "He did evil in the eyes of the LORD" (2 Kings 13:2 NIV). If it is wearisome to the reader to come across this little refrain every few chapters, think how dreary and tiring it must have been for God to watch one scion of David after another squander his moments on the stage of history in petty graft, idolatry, and pandering after foreign influences.

So when a name like *Hezekiah* sounds out in the roll call of the book of Kings, everyone's head snaps to attention. We know a different story is coming now. Here's a man who, from the moment he took the throne at age twenty-five, did what was right in God's eyes. He "destroyed the local shrines, then tore down the images of foreign gods and cut down the sacred pole for worshiping the goddess Asherah. He also smashed the bronze snake Moses had made. The people had named it Nehushtan and had been offering sacrifices to it" (2 Kings 18:4 CEV).

Hezekiah's spiritual housecleaning of Judah—and the northern territories of Israel after that nation had collapsed—was so thorough and so radical that even the invading Assyrian emperor Sennacherib heard of it, though he misunderstood what Hezekiah was doing.

We learn about Sennacherib's misjudgment through a speech his mouthpiece, Rabshakeh, made (while Sennacherib himself was a few miles away tearing down the walls of another Judean city). Rabshakeh challenged Hezekiah and the Hebrew people, raising his voice to a booming pitch so he could be heard even by the crowd watching the scene from the city walls. He threatened the people with menacing images of total destruction, as the Assyrians had already inflicted on many other cities.

Sennacherib then tried to preempt Hezekiah's hope that Israel's God would save her, by sending a letter by messenger: "Don't be deceived by your god. He can't save you. Remember, you cut down all those altars and worship places all over this land, the places where people could worship the god that protects this land. Now your goose is cooked, because no god has been able to withstand me yet, and yours won't be able to either!"

He shouldn't have said that. Hezekiah, king of Judah, was a staunch fan of the God of Israel. And because of Hezekiah's faith, Israel's God was a great fan of his too. So Hezekiah brought the letter to the temple in Jerusalem. He spread it out before God and prayed his heart out.

Hezekiah soon heard back from God, via the prophet Isaiah. "These so-called threats? I *laugh* at them," God assured him. "Don't worry about this. I'll take care of it."

And he did! The army of the Assyrians, 185,000 strong, was camped in a circle surrounding the city of Jerusalem. The Bible reports: "And it came to pass on a certain night that the angel of the LORD went out, and killed in the camp of the Assyrians one hundred and eighty-five thousand; and when people arose early in the morning, there were the corpses—all dead" (2 Kings 19:35 NKJV). Sennacherib slunk back to Assyria without the conquering army he'd set out with. And a defenseless emperor was soon a dead emperor.

Hezekiah apparently knew the exhilaration of a life that had some extreme high points and some extreme low points. What helped him keep his head screwed on tight and his heart directed rightly on that roller-coaster ride of a life he led was that he consistently and enthusiastically served his God.

To read more about Hezekiah and Sennacherib, see 2 Kings 18–19 (and the parallel story in 2 Chronicles 32:1–23 and Isaiah 36–37).

Well of Woes

Jeremiah Escapes from a Well

OLD TESTAMENT PROPHETS were usually more *in*famous than famous. Their messages from God netted them beatings, reprimands by kings, death threats, and—sadly—*carried-out* death sentences.

Jeremiah was one of the most beleaguered prophets in Judah, the southern kingdom of Israel. Called as a prophet during a time of intense political upheaval, he had the thankless task of warning the people about the consequences of their rebellion toward God. The consequences involved siege, famine, and invasion by enemy forces.

At this point, Jeremiah was under house arrest at the word of Zedekiah—the king of Judah appointed by Nebuchadnezzar, the king of Babylon, whose army had Jerusalem under siege. During a temporary cease-fire due to the arrival of Israel's allies—the Egyptian army—Jeremiah angered many palace officials with his prophecy that the Babylonians would soon conquer Jerusalem. They were especially angry when he told them to surrender to the Babylonians! In their eyes this was treason.

Beating Jeremiah and arresting him simply were not enough to keep him from saying what the people didn't want to hear. So palace officials suggested the ultimate solution to Zedekiah: Jeremiah must die. "It's the only way to silence him," they reasoned.

Zedekiah was never a king viewed as a tower of strength. He allowed the officials to do whatever they liked to Jeremiah. And what they liked was to have him thrown into a muddy, waterless well, where he would eventually starve to death.

So down he went.

But there was one palace official who didn't go along with the program. This man, Ebed-Melech, complained to the king on behalf of Jeremiah. "What those men did to Jeremiah was wrong," he said. "If Jeremiah stays in that well, he'll die of hunger."

Zedekiah took Ebed-Melech's words to heart. Finally, he allowed Ebed-Melech to take a group of men and lift Jeremiah out of the well. But first, he needed a few supplies, namely old clothes.

The plan was this: The rescuers would lower the clothes to Jeremiah to place around his arms to protect them against the rope's friction. The men would then lift him out of the well. Finally, inch by careful inch, Jeremiah was lifted out of the well. Although he was taken back to the same prison as before, at least it wasn't a muddy one.

To read more about Jeremiah's well of woes, read Jeremiah 38:1–13.

A Hot Time in
the Old Town Tonight

Daniel's Friends Escape a Fiery Death

EVER EXPERIENCED A TIME when a bad situation turned into an even worse one? Shadrach, Meshach, and Abednego, three exiles from Israel, found themselves in such a bad-to-worse situation.

During the time of Israel's exile in Babylon, Daniel, Shadrach, Meshach, and Abednego were fish out of water in a strange land far from home. Blessed with exceptional looks and intelligence, the four young men were accepted into a training program that ended in service to Nebuchadnezzar, the king of the conquering nation of Babylon. They eventually rose to positions of authority in the land (see Daniel 1–2). While their situation so far was not so bad, life was about to take a dangerous turn.

Nebuchadnezzar had a huge golden idol set up in a place where all could see it. At certain times of the day, music would be played. During those times, all were to worship the golden idol. Those who refused would be thrown into a hot furnace. There were no exceptions to this rule.

When anyone rises quickly to power, you can be sure that others notice. Chaldean men who probably envied the success of Shadrach, Meshach, and Abednego quickly informed the king of Shadrach, Meshach, and Abednego's refusal to worship the golden idol.

Not wasting any time, Nebuchadnezzar had the three men summoned into his presence and demanded to know whether or not they dared to ignore the decree to worship the gods of the Babylonians. He would even give them another chance to worship the idol when the music played. If they didn't, they would be tossed into the furnace, and no one could save them.

But instead of bowing down, Shadrach, Meshach, and Abednego told him, "If our God Whom we serve is able to deliver us from the burning fiery furnace, He will deliver us out of your hand, O king. But if not, let it be known to you, O king, that we will not serve your gods or worship the golden image which you have set up!" (Daniel 3:17–18 AMP).

These brave words only inspired Nebuchadnezzar to fury. Not only did he have the three men thrown into the furnace, he demanded that it be heated seven times hotter than normal. So hot was this furnace that the people charged with throwing them into it were killed simply by being near it!

You might think that was the end of the story—three men martyred for their faith. But that was not the end. Nebuchadnezzar witnessed an amazing sight: Not only were Shadrach, Meshach, and Abednego still alive in the furnace, they were not the only ones present. A fourth man stood with them! The fourth man looked "like a son of the gods" (Daniel 3:25). Was this God himself or an angel he sent to stand with his faithful followers? Regardless of who it was, God showed that he indeed could save his people.

Nebuchadnezzar, still not a man to waste time, had Shadrach, Meshach, and Abednego brought out of the furnace. And he was inspired by the three men to make a new law: anyone who spoke against the God of Shadrach, Meshach, and Abednego would be put to death!

Shadrach, Meshach, and Abednego's fiery adventure is found in Daniel 3.

MAJOR EMPIRES OF BIBLE TIMES

There were many world powers when Israel grew as a nation. Consequently, Israel made allies and enemies.

EMPIRE	LEADER[S]
Amalekites	Agag, the king Saul was supposed to kill (1 Samuel 15)
Ammonites	Unnamed king whom Jephthah defeated (Judges 11:4–33) Nahash, who was defeated by Saul (1 Samuel 11:1–11) Hanun, who reacted badly to a delegation sent by David (2 Samuel 10:1–14) Baalis, who sent an assassin to kill Gedaliah, governor of Judah (Jeremiah 40:14)
Assyrians	Tiglath-pileser III, who captured Israelites and took them to Assyria (2 Kings 15:29; 16:7–10) Shalmaneser V, who attacked Hoshea, king of Israel, and captured Samaria (2 Kings 17:1–6; 18:9–11) Sennacherib, who attacked Judah (2 Kings 18:13–19:37) Esarhaddon, who captured King Manasseh (2 Kings 19:37; 2 Chronicles 33:11) Ashurbanipal, who probably freed King Manasseh (Ezra 4:10)

Empire	Leader[s]
Babylonians	Merodach-Baladan, who sent a delegation to visit Hezekiah (2 Kings 20:12; Isaiah 39:1) Evil-Merodach, who released Jehoiachin from prison (2 Kings 25:27; Jeremiah 52:31) Nebuchadnezzar, whose dreams were interpreted by Daniel (2 Kings 24–25; 2 Chronicles 36; Daniel 1–4) Belshazzar, who saw the handwriting on the wall (Daniel 5)
Canaanites	Bera, the king of Sodom, who was captured with Lot and later rescued by Abram (Genesis 14:1–24) Unnamed king of Arad who attacked the Israelites in the Negev (Numbers 21:1–3) Unnamed king of Jericho when the city fell (Joshua 2:2) Adoni-Zedek, king of Jerusalem defeated by Joshua and the army of Israel (Joshua 10:1–27) Jabin, king of Hazor defeated by Joshua and the army of Israel (Joshua 11:1–11) Jabin, another king of Hazor, whose army commander, Sisera, was killed by Jael (Judges 4:2–23)
Edomites	Unnamed king who did not want Israel to pass through his land (Numbers 20:14–21)

EMPIRE	LEADER[S]
Egyptians	Various pharaohs, including: —the pharaoh with whom Abraham dealt (Genesis 12:10–20) —the pharaoh for whom Joseph served as second-in-command (Genesis 39–50) —the pharaoh who knew nothing about Joseph, enslaved the Hebrew people, and called for all newborn male babies to be thrown into the Nile River (Exodus 1:8–11; Acts 7:18) —the pharaoh who sought to kill Moses (possibly Thutmose III—Exodus 2:11–23) —Amenhotep II, with whom Moses dealt during the plagues (Exodus 5–14) —the pharaoh whose daughter Solomon married (1 Kings 3:1) —Shishak, who attacked King Rehoboam (1 Kings 14:25–26) —Neco, who killed King Josiah of Judah at the battle of Megiddo (2 Kings 23:29–30; Jeremiah 46:1–26) —Hophra, against whom Jeremiah prophesied (Jeremiah 44:30)

EMPIRE	LEADER[S]
Medes and Persians	Cyrus the Great, who allowed some exiles to return to Jerusalem (2 Chronicles 36:22–23; Ezra 1–6; Isaiah 44:28–45:13; 48:14; Daniel 6:28; 10:1) Darius the Mede, who allowed Daniel to be thrown into the lions' den (Daniel 6) Darius the Great, who allowed the people to continue rebuilding the temple (Ezra 5–6) Ahasuerus (Xerxes), who married Esther (the book of Esther) Artaxerxes, whom Nehemiah served as cupbearer (Ezra 7:1; Nehemiah 2:1–9)
Moabites	Balak, who wanted the Israelites cursed (Numbers 22–24) Eglon, who was killed by Ehud (Judges 3:12–30) Mesha, who rebelled against Israel (2 Kings 3:4–27)
Philistines	Abimelech, to whom Abraham lied about Sarah (Genesis 20) and to whom Isaac lied about Rebekah (Genesis 26) Achish, king in Gath who thought David was insane at first but later welcomed him (1 Samuel 21:10–15; 27–29)

EMPIRE	LEADER[S]
Romans	Ruled by emperors like: —Caesar Augustus (Luke 2:1—the time of Jesus' birth) —Tiberius Caesar (Luke 3:1—the time of John the Baptist's ministry) —Claudius Caesar (Acts 11:28—the time of a great famine; Acts 18:2—he expelled the Jews from Rome) —Nero Caesar (Acts 25:10–12—the emperor at the time of Paul's appeal to Rome)
Syrians (Arameans)	Hazael, whom Elijah was told to anoint as king of Syria; he later murdered Ben-Hadad II (1 Kings 19:15–17; 2 Kings 8–13) Ben-Hadad I, the king of Syria who attacked Samaria during the time of Ahab (1 Kings 20:1–34) Ben-Hadad II who sent Naaman to Israel to be cured of leprosy (2 Kings 5:1–6) Rezin, king of Syria who besieged Ahaz (2 Kings 16:5–9)
Tyrians	Hiram, who made a treaty with Solomon (1 Kings 5) Prince of Tyre (Ezekiel 28:1–10)

Escape to Egypt

Herod Carries Out a Grisly Prophecy While Jesus Escapes

THE AMAZING THING about prophecies—real prophecies from God, rather than those made up by people—is that they come true. They cannot be thwarted. We see it all the time in stories where the villain tries to prevent a prophecy of his or her downfall from coming to pass by killing the one destined to bring about that downfall. Well, many of those stories were inspired by the true story of Jesus—the child that King Herod wanted to murder.

In Matthew 2:1–12 we read that Herod sent the Magi to Bethlehem to seek the Messiah. Micah, an Old Testament prophet who lived hundreds of years earlier, had announced that Bethlehem was the birthplace of the Savior—the one the Magi called a king (see Micah 5:2).

But God had other plans for the Magi that didn't involve returning to Jerusalem to report on Jesus' probable whereabouts. Having used a dream to warn the Magi to escape, God used another dream to warn Joseph, the earthly father of Jesus, to take his family and escape to Egypt. Joseph and his family were to remain there until God gave the word for them to return.

Joseph didn't wait till morning. He took his family and escaped that night, thus fulfilling a prophecy of Hosea: "I called my son out of Egypt" (Hosea 11:1 NLT).

Meanwhile, back in Jerusalem, Herod was cooling his heels, waiting for the Magi to return—a fruitless wait. With his anger at the boiling point, Herod decided to have all the boys two years of age and under in Bethlehem killed, thinking that at last he would rid himself of any young rivals.

As we mentioned in the first paragraph, prophecies come true. Sadly, the death of children was prophesied hundreds of years earlier by the prophet Jeremiah: "A cry is heard in Ramah—deep anguish and bitter weeping. Rachel weeps for her children, refusing to be comforted—for her children are gone" (Jeremiah 31:15 NLT).

But Herod could not kill Jesus. Once Herod died, God used a dream to guide Joseph and his family out of Egypt. Taking no chances, Joseph settled in Nazareth, thus fulfilling yet another prophecy concerning Jesus—that he would be called a Nazarene (see Matthew 2:23 NLT).

That's the thing about real prophecies. They always come true.

The Story of Jesus' escape to Egypt can be found in Matthew 2:13–23.

A Real Basket Case

When Threatened with Death, Saul (Paul) Escapes in a Basket

WE'VE ALL READ stories about ingenious escapes involving someone being lowered out of a window. But any fictional escapade takes a backseat to the real-life story of Saul (later called Paul).

For Saul, Christians were the enemies, and he had the authority of the Jewish ruling council to do something about them. But while on his way to collect and imprison a group of Christians, he heard the voice of the last person he ever thought he would hear—that of the risen Christ.

Instead of asking Saul why he persecuted believers, Jesus helped Saul understand that Saul was actually persecuting Jesus. That experience on the road to the walled city of Damascus made Saul a Christ-follower—something he could not have imagined being the day before.

But now Saul had a problem—the encounter with Jesus rendered him totally blind. He had to be led into Damascus. There he received a momentous visit from a believer named Ananias.

What prompted this visit was a vision from God telling Ananias to find Saul. But Ananias was afraid to face Saul. Hadn't Saul persecuted Christians? Going to see Saul was like putting a noose around your neck. But God refused to take no for an answer. As he explained to Ananias, Saul was the tool he would use to draw Gentiles into his kingdom.

Ananias soon found Saul and healed him of blindness. With his spiritual blindness also healed, Saul became filled with the Holy Spirit.

Now that Saul was a believer, he eagerly preached in the synagogues, gaining followers. But his conversion earned him enemies among the Jews. For them, Saul was now a problem that only his death could solve. And best of all, Saul was trapped in the walled city of Damascus! They kept watch, waiting for just the right moment. If he tried to step through the city gates, they would have him. Perhaps Saul could see the irony of the situation, now that he was caught in the web he might have woven around the believers of the city had he not met Jesus.

But there was a way out. Saul's followers had a plan of their own—one involving a basket. In the dead of the night, they placed Saul in a large basket and carefully lowered him through a hole in the city wall.

Imagine how Saul felt as the basket moved lower and lower. Would this work? Would he survive this escape attempt?

Saul survived and wound up in Jerusalem, where he later met Barnabas, a disciple who would one day travel with Saul on his missionary journeys. But that's another story.

To read about Saul's exciting adventure, read Acts 9:20–25.

PART FIVE

Curious Crimes

Unfriendly Fire

Aaron's Sons Die Instantly When They Use the Wrong Kind of Fire

THE REALITY OF THE POWER and holiness of the Lord is never more emphasized than through stories like that of Nadab and Abihu.

When God established the priesthood among the people of Israel, he first gave the job to Aaron and his sons (see Exodus 28:1) and later to others from the tribe of Levi (see Deuteronomy 10:8). Aaron served as the first high priest of Israel. A priest made offerings to the Lord to atone for the sins of the people. The law of Moses included the kinds of offerings—whether animal, vegetable, or mineral—acceptable to the Lord for specific sins.

Since the priest stood in the tabernacle as the representative of Israel before a holy God, everything had to be done right. The priests had to wear the special linen garments designed for them, which included bells at the hem. Entering God's presence flippantly could be deadly. The bells were not used to provide background music. Their presence signaled only one thing: if the people stopped hearing the bells, that meant the priest was dead.

This was a sobering thought, one made all the more real in the story of Nadab and Abihu, Aaron's oldest sons. On a typical day in which the two priests placed fire in censers used for burning incense, a very atypical thing happened: the fire of God flashed out, killing them instantly.

How could such a terrible thing happen? And why?

The fire was deemed "unauthorized" (Leviticus 10:1 NIV), which meant that the Lord did not sanction the use of it. Does that mean they used the wrong coals or took fire from the wrong place (for example, a place other than the altar of incense)? While the text does not clearly state why this fire was "unauthorized," the sad fact remains that somehow the men became careless in their actions. But priests could not afford to be careless when working around the holy things of the tabernacle. This is why Moses shared the following message from God to a grieving Aaron: "Among those who approach me I will show myself holy; in the sight of all the people I will be honored" (Leviticus 10:3). The actions of Nadab and Abihu dishonored God.

Not only that, God commanded Aaron *not* to mourn for his sons in the traditional way—tearing his clothes and showing other visible signs of grief. While God's words through Moses might sound cruel or inhumane (especially since Nadab and Abihu were Moses' nephews), they were a reminder that the high priest was God's man. Aaron's sons made light of God's holiness and suffered the consequences—death. To wildly grieve in the sight of Israel would have sent the message that God was in the wrong for what he did.

But Aaron's family members were allowed to mourn for their kin. Some of Aaron's relatives were given the responsibility of carrying out the bodies and leaving them outside the camp of Israel.

Afterward, God told Aaron and his sons to avoid the use of alcohol while working in the tabernacle. Perhaps this warning was a statement about why Nadab and Abihu grew careless. Regardless, the takeaway of the tragedy was this: never take lightly the holiness of God.

To read more about this tragedy, read Leviticus 10:1–11 and Numbers 3:1–4.

Between a Rock
and a Hard Place

When Moses Gets Angry, Hard Consequences Result

SOMETIMES LOSING one's temper can have long-lasting consequences. But even the most godly people can sometimes lose their tempers. Moses, one of the greatest prophets and the man to whom God handed the Ten Commandments, messed up royally when he found himself between a rock in a very hard place.

The walk from Egypt to the Promised Land of Canaan proved to be anything but a walk in the park for the often beleaguered Moses. Imagine walking through a desert with enough people— enough *grumbling* people—to fill a large city, even by today's population standards. Whenever the people of Israel lacked something, they were quick to let Moses know about it. As the ranking leader of the expedition, Moses was in the hot seat of blame. The gist of their complaints were as follows:

"Moses, we don't have any food. It's your fault."

"Moses, we don't have any water. It's your fault."

"Moses, we should never have left Egypt. At least we had food there. Why did you make us? It's your fault."

Imagine forty years of that!

Now, on one particular day in the Desert of Zin, the people grumbled about their lack of water. No surprises there. Deserts don't tend to have an abundance of water in convenient places. So

Moses and his brother, Aaron—another candidate for blame—went to the tabernacle to ask God for help.

God had a solution for the water shortage: take Aaron's rod and speak to a rock to receive water. While this command might sound strange, years previously, God told Moses to strike a rock with the staff and water would come out of it (see Exodus 17:1–7).

With staff in hand, Moses and Aaron approached the appointed rock while the people waited with breathless anticipation. But instead of speaking to the rock, a fed-up Moses angrily struck the rock with the staff, saying, "Listen, you rebels, must we bring you water out of this rock?" (Numbers 20:10 NIV).

Sounds just a wee bit prideful.

Although God honored Moses' request for water, he had hard words for his prophet: "Because you did not trust in me enough to honor me as holy in the sight of the Israelites, you will not bring this community into the land I give them" (Numbers 20:12).

You have only to read Deuteronomy 32:48–52 and 34:1–8 to learn that Moses died just before the people of Israel entered the Promised Land. He had had one temper tantrum too many.

Numbers 20:1–13 has the story of Moses and the rock.

A Stab in the Dark

Ehud, a Left-Handed Judge, Kills Eglon, the Moabite King

MOST ADVENTURE STORIES involve a hero (male or female) and a villain. The conflict comes when their goals clash. Think about the hero Luke Skywalker in the *Star Wars* series. In one episode he had a clash with villain Jabba the Hutt, a six-hundred-year-old crime lord most known for his enormous girth. The guy was seriously fat. Think that situation is too fantastic to believe? Well, listen to this story. Sometimes truth is stranger than fiction.

During a long period of Israel's history, before the advent of the kings, judges ruled the people of Israel. Throughout the book of Judges, the stories of the judges are punctuated by a similar epitaph: "The Israelites did evil in the LORD's sight" (Judges 6:1 NLT). As a result of Israel's tendency to wander, the Lord allowed her enemies to grow strong and cause misery for the Israelites. But he had pity on his people as well and chose judges to lead the people against their enemies. The judges acted as military leaders and advisers to the people of Israel. Names such as Samson, Deborah, and Gideon probably sound familiar. But what about Ehud? We'll get to him in a minute. First, let's talk about the villain of the piece.

One of the prime legislators of misery was Eglon, king of the Moabites—one of Israel's bitterest enemies. Eglon was the Jabba the Hutt of his day and was probably every bit as cruel in the eighteen years that he lorded it over Israel. It's not often that the Bible provides information about the weight of an individual. But we're told almost right away that Eglon "was very fat" (Judges 3:17). Why the mention of weight? It proved to have a bearing on the action in the story.

A conquered nation usually had to provide a tribute to the conquerors. You know—gold, jewels, spices—whatever they had of value. During this time frame, God chose Ehud to be a judge of Israel to rescue them from King Eglon and the Moabites. His task was to present the tribute to Eglon. But Ehud had a surprising secret: he was left-handed. While that might not seem like an earth-shattering trait to make the headlines, it spelled disaster for Eglon. Here's how it went down.

Having been chosen to deliver the tribute, Ehud equipped himself with a double-edged sword, one that would cut in any direction it faced, which he could swiftly draw from the right by using his left hand. Obviously, he didn't plan to just make his delivery to Eglon and then be on his way!

While Ehud's sword didn't have the lineage or the length of Luke Skywalker's light saber, it did the trick. With the tribute delivered, Ehud went into action. The king foolishly sent away all of his attendants in the hopes of hearing a secret message from Ehud in private. Bad move, Eglon. If this were part of the *Star Wars* movies, the tempo of the music would kick up a notch to underline the suspense. Cool as a cucumber, Ehud drew his sword from its hiding place under his clothes and left it where it landed—in Eglon's stomach—before escaping. The Bible provides the added detail that the sword "disappeared beneath the king's fat." Just when you thought the story couldn't get any grosser . . .

Ehud locked the doors and escaped the scene. He went back to the Hebrew people and sounded the alarm. "Follow me," he said, "for the LORD has given you victory over Moab your enemy." The people went to battle, and "Moab was conquered by Israel that day, and there was peace in the land for eighty years" (Judges 3:28, 30).

Hollywood probably won't make Ehud's story into a movie, but the plot is similar to many offerings. Bad king meets bad end at the hand of good guy. And throwing in a little bit of gross never hurt either.

Read Ehud's story in Judges 3:12–30.

Untouchable

A Man Touches the Ark of the Covenant and Dies on the Spot

THE DECLARATION OF INDEPENDENCE is housed under bulletproof glass to protect this delicate document. For Americans, it is a symbol of our national covenant. The ark of the covenant housed the symbols of the Israelites' covenant with God—the tablets of the Ten Commandments. The ark was a symbol of the throne of God—the King of the earth. This holy object was just as untouchable as the Declaration of Independence behind its bulletproof glass. Holy objects were not to be treated lightly. Only the priests could carry the ark, and only by holding poles inserted into the rings. It was not to be touched (see Numbers 4:4–6, 15).

During the time of the prophet Samuel, the Philistines—the perennial disrupters of joy for the people of Israel—stole the ark and took it to the city of Ashdod (see 1 Samuel 4–5). God struck the people of Ashdod with a plague, so they did the smart thing—they tried to give the ark back to Israel, along with a peace offering. After about seventy people died because they looked in the ark, it was taken to the home of Abinadab, where it remained for twenty years (see 1 Samuel 6:1–7:2).

When David became king over Israel, he decided to bring the ark back to Jerusalem. With an honor guard of about thirty thousand, David arrived to escort the ark. They made a celebration out of it, with worship music at full blast.

Problem was, no one consulted the manual about how to transport the ark. So they put it on a cart pulled by oxen.

Wrong.

While the ark traveled on a new cart, the unthinkable happened. One of the oxen pulling it slipped for some reason. Without stopping to think about it, a man named Uzzah reached out to steady the ark, and God put him to death on the spot.

Uzzah's death was unsettling for David. Instead of bringing the ark back to Jerusalem, he left it in the home of a Levite named Obed-Edom for a few months. But those few months proved a bounty for Obed-Edom and his family because of the ark's presence.

Hearing that Obed-Edom's family was blessed for having the ark rather than cursed, David finally had enough nerve to complete the ark's journey.

But this time, he read the instruction manual.

To find out more about the ark's rocky road to Jerusalem, read 2 Samuel 6.

Off with His Head

When John the Baptist Speaks Out Against Herod, Heads Roll

OUTSPOKEN PROPHETS had a low survival rate in Bible times. They often stepped on the toes of kings and other leaders by confronting them about bad behavior at God's command. Consequently, many wished to see the prophets dead.

John the Baptist had always been outspoken. The first time we hear of him is in Matthew 3, where he preached in the Judean wilderness. Numerous people went to hear him speak, wondering whether he was the promised Messiah. But he was the herald of the Messiah—Jesus—and one who didn't shy away from calling the Pharisees and Sadducees a "brood of snakes" (Matthew 3:7 MSG). John was an "Elijah" that Malachi prophesied would come to earth to change the people's hearts toward each other (see Malachi 4:5–6). John the Baptist confronted wrong wherever he found it.

So it should have come as no surprise that John would confront the ruler of Galilee, Herod Antipas, about his marriage to Herodias. Herodias had been married to Herod's brother Philip but left him for Herod. This action was unlawful according to the law of Moses (see Leviticus 18:16). Well, Herod couldn't be bothered with all that, and he threw John into prison. He was reluctant to kill John since he had the favor of the people. But Herodias had other plans.

One night, during a party to celebrate Herod's birthday, Herodias's daughter, Salome, performed a dance before Herod and his guests. This must have been some dance, because Herod swore an oath that he would give her anything she wanted. A rash promise. Herodias had already coached her daughter on what to say: "Give me the head of John the Baptist here on a platter" (Matthew 14:8 ESV). Shades of the Queen of Hearts in *Alice in Wonderland*.

Herod instantly regretted making such a promise. But because he wanted to save face in front of his guests and had given his word, he ordered the execution. John was beheaded in prison, and his head was placed on a tray and handed to Herodias's daughter, who gave it to her mother. Later, John's disciples buried John's body.

To his chagrin, Herod may have won that round, but ultimately he lost more than he won. One day he would have to face the judgment of God.

To read more about John the Baptist's confrontation of Herod Antipas, see Matthew 14:1–12 and Luke 3:19–20.

Heinous Harvest

Jesus' Disciples Pick a Peck of Problems

MANY STATES have really odd laws still on their books that we might find strange. For example, an internet website mentions that it is illegal in Alabama to wear a fake mustache that causes people to laugh in church. In Texas you're not allowed to put graffiti on a cow owned by someone else. Yep, odd laws.

But who would have thought that picking grain would be considered unlawful? And who would have thought that *Jesus' disciples* would be guilty of that "crime"? Here's the story.

While walking with Jesus through a grain field, the disciples discovered they were pretty hungry. After all, there were no grocery stores back in their time. So they plucked the grain to eat.

The Pharisees, the always-present clouds of judgment, happened to notice the disciples picking the grain. Ah, now they had something to accuse Jesus of—picking grain on a Sabbath. Work of any kind was unlawful on the Sabbath. The Pharisees could easily quote the law, which stated: "Remember the Sabbath day by keeping it holy. Six days you shall labor and do all your work, but the seventh day is a Sabbath to the LORD your God. On it you shall not do any work, neither you, nor your son or daughter, nor your manservant or maidservant, nor your animals, nor the alien within your gates" (Exodus 20:8–10 NIV).

But Jesus reminded the Pharisees of the precedent set by David during Old Testament times. While on the run from Saul, David and his men ate the bread left as an offering to God in the tabernacle—the bread that only priests usually ate (see 1 Samuel 21:1–6).

But the main issue for Jesus was the lack of grace the Pharisees showed. As the Son of God, he was really the one in charge of the Sabbath. That meant *he* made the rules concerning the Sabbath. And his rule was mercy. He reminded the Pharisees of the words God spoke through the prophet Hosea: "I desire mercy, not sacrifice" (Hosea 6:6 NIV).

So were the disciples guilty as charged? In a legalistic society, yes. But a merciful God said no.

Matthew 12:1–8 has the scoop on this unusual crime.

Caught in the Act

Jesus Pardons a Woman Caught in the Act of Adultery

TODAY MANY LESS-THAN-STELLAR CRIMINALS have been "caught on tape" in videos made by enterprising videographers who just happened to catch someone in the middle of a crime. Back in Jesus' day, catching someone in the act of a crime earned many a person a death sentence.

One day, while Jesus was about to teach the people in the temple courts, some of the Jewish leaders brought a woman before him. Apparently, she'd been caught in an adulterous act—a crime punishable by death. As the law stated, "If a man commits adultery with his neighbor's wife, both the man and the woman who have committed adultery must be put to death" (Leviticus 20:10 NLT; see also Deuteronomy 22:22). So the religious leaders wondered, *What will Jesus do in this situation?*

You don't have to be a *Law and Order* expert to know that those who brought the woman before Jesus had her dead to rights, especially because the act had been witnessed (see Deuteronomy 19:15). So what was wrong with this picture? Three things really, which Jesus was quick to see: (1) an act of adultery takes two people; where was the man who was also involved? (2) as a people under the authority of Rome, the Israelites no longer had the authority to carry out executions; and (3) the fact that the woman was brought to Jesus shows that this was a no-win situation designed to trap him. If he said, "Go ahead and stone her," they could accuse him of conspiring against the Romans, which could earn *him* a death sentence.

If he said, "Don't stone her," they could accuse him of ignoring the law.

What the Jewish leaders didn't take into account was Jesus' wisdom. He did the very thing no one expected him to do: he began to write on the ground instead of answering their question. After a while, he made a statement that many have quoted long afterward: "Let him who is without sin among you be the first to throw a stone at her" (John 8:7 AMP).

We may never know what Jesus wrote on the ground, since the Bible does not say. Some have speculated that he wrote the sins of those present. Whatever he wrote, his words had an impact on the crowd, which slowly dispersed, leaving only the woman standing before Jesus.

Imagine how the woman felt when she saw that her accusers had vanished. Imagine also her feelings when Jesus said the words that many accused and broken under the weight of judgment have always longed to hear: "I do not condemn you either. Go on your way and from now on sin no more" (John 8:11). He had given her the gift of a second chance.

Read this unusual exchange in John 8:1–11.

A King Crucified

Jesus Is Crucified for Calling Himself a King

FOR MOST OF HIS LIFE, Jesus lived and ministered quietly, going out of his way to avoid being detected. Ironically, when he did finally announce that he was the long-awaited promised one, the heir to David's throne, he was rejected. Go figure.

People desperately wanted him to be the Jewish Messiah; they sometimes tried to forcibly make him king. In the stories that have Galilee as their backdrop, it often looked like a game of hide-and-seek as Jesus criss-crossed the lake in various boats and the crowds shuffled around the edge of the lake to keep up with him. Perhaps it was precisely *because* he knew their fickle hearts that Jesus evaded the title "king" as long as he could. We can look back and see what happened once the truth was out; very likely, Jesus *foresaw* it.

During the last week of his earthly life and ministry, Jesus entered Jerusalem, accompanied by unavoidable clamor—flowers, palm branches, and clothes strewn in the path before him. Children shouted out "Hosanna!" and his wide circle of provisionally committed disciples shouted, "Blessed is He who comes in the name of the LORD. The King of Israel!" (John 12:13 NKJV). The very same crowd would shout "Crucify Him, crucify Him!" only a few days later (John 19:6).

The secret was out. For the next few days, Jesus acted as one who was "known" as a candidate for messiahship. His relationships with religious authorities immediately became very frosty, at least on their part. For his part, Jesus demonstrated that he indeed had the authority to rule—but they all misunderstood what kind of king-dom he would have.

As the week wound to a close, Jesus had his last meal with the disciples and then was arrested in the Garden of Gethsemane. From the moment of Judas's treacherous kiss (see "The Kiss of Death," p. 113), Jesus calmly met the fate for which he had come to earth in the first place.

The synoptic Gospels—Matthew, Mark, and Luke—focus more on the interrogations by the high priests and Jewish authorities in which Jesus' claims to messiahship were directly challenged and ul-timately rejected.

The Gospel of John, on the other hand, gives us a different point of view. It provides a longer look at the Roman governor's de-liberations as he pondered the unique prisoner sent to him. John shows us Pilate's increasingly troubled frame of mind as he realized that so much more was going on with Jesus' claim to be King of the Jews than his rationalistic Roman soul had ever considered before. Pilate tried to free Jesus and kept asking the Jews, "Shall I crucify your King?" However, the religious leaders who had gotten them-selves all into a lather answered, "We have no king but Caesar!" (John 19:15).

So Jesus was soon hanging on a cross, dripping out his life blood, under a sign that read, "Jesus of Nazareth, the King of the Jews" in each of the three languages known and spoken by most people of that day. The finagling back and forth between Pilate, who would have liked to avoid the open confrontation, and the Jewish authorities, who also would have preferred not to give Jesus so much publicity, actually resulted in defeating both purposes. But not God's purposes. "This man was handed over to you by God's set purpose and foreknowledge" the apostle Peter said a few weeks later, "and you, with the help of wicked men, put him to death by nailing him to the cross" (Acts 2:23 NIV).

Jesus was crucified for claiming to be a king. Before he went to his death, he said to Pilate, "You are right in saying I am a king. In fact, for this reason I was born, and for this I came into the world, to testify to the truth. Everyone on the side of truth listens to me" (John 18:37 NIV).

What was true that day is still true today.

To read more about Jesus' claims to kingship, face-to-face with Pilate, read John 18:29–19:22.

A Harmful Healing

Peter and John Are Arrested for Healing a Man

THE APOSTLES were on a roll. A lot of things had been going their way for several weeks now. Thousands of believers had been added to the newly gathered band of Jesus followers. They lived in harmony with one another, sharing meals, prayer needs, and every sort of joy and sorrow. Best of all, the apparent motive of all this was a genuine love, both for the Messiah Jesus and for their fellow believers. The tensions they had experienced between Jesus and the Jewish religious leaders—the hierarchy that had never sanctioned Jesus' ministry—were now mostly a repressed memory. Or so they thought.

After Jesus' departure heavenward, the disciples were, as the closing verse of Luke's gospel describes it, "in the Temple all the time, praising God" (Luke 24:53 NCV). As the place where God's name and presence was most visibly represented on earth, the temple at Jerusalem seemed the right place for the new messianic movement to have its center.

So one day Peter and John were going up as usual to enter the temple for the 3:00 p.m. prayers. As they passed through the Beautiful Gate, they saw a man lying there begging for alms. He'd been brought to that place at that time nearly all his life, for he'd been crippled since birth. Had Peter seen him before? Most certainly. Perhaps every day.

But something felt different today. Peter and John were, as we already said, on a roll. Each day they kept seeing greater and greater signs of the power of Jesus working through them, and this day Peter felt the Spirit inspiring him to do something extraordinary. He called and got the man's attention, and something about Peter's deliberateness brought the man to focus upon him and John.

"Now, I don't have any money to give you," Peter began, which must have given the poor guy pause.

What? Well, what are you going to do, then? the crippled man maybe thought. *Give me one of those little rolled-up "tracts" to read later? Pray some long and sanctimonious prayer over me, embarrassing me all the more as you call attention to my hopeless condition?*

But before the man even knew what had happened, Peter reached down, grabbed hold of his hand, and pulled him upright to a standing position. At the same time he said, as someone convinced of the truth of it, "I do have something else I can give you. By the power of Jesus Christ from Nazareth, stand up and walk!" (Acts 3:6 NCV). And to the man's everlasting astonishment, he did.

He found himself standing on two strong legs, legs that had never practiced walking a single step in his entire life but which now of their own accord took him running down the stone walkway, wheeling around, racing back, and then leaping high into the air, where he whooped and hollered. "I'm walking! I'm running! I'm leaping into the air! Praise be to God Almighty!"

He kept yelling and praising God and making such a clamor

that everyone ran to see what had happened. Peter, of course, took the opportunity to call attention to Jesus and what he offers those who will trust and obey him. And a most persuasive example trembled and bobbed beside Peter. He intermittently leapt into the air like a jackrabbit, yahooing and praising the Lord Jesus Christ, who had made him whole after more than forty years of miserable and useless days lying helpless and dependent on others.

But just as the party was getting merry, the Joy Police showed up (the high priests, Sadducees, and temple guard). With great annoyance, they arrested the apostles and hustled them off the scene to a back room somewhere to let them cool their heels overnight.

Since when was healing a lame man considered a felony? No matter which way you tried to turn this one over, it didn't make sense. The next day, when the haughty temple leaders called forth the men to interrogate them further, the absurdity of trying to "press charges" on Peter and John for healing a man crippled for forty years, or on the man himself for leaping and praising God in the temple districts, became obvious. They realized they really couldn't make any kind of charges stick, so they just warned them, "Don't do anything like this again!"

Yeah, right.

To read more about this joyous event, see Acts 3:1–4:22.

The Exorcist

Paul Is Arrested for Healing a Demon-Possessed Girl

NVRDLMMNT. "NEVER A DULL MOMENT." Paul could have put that on his license plate. Wherever he went, it seems that trouble always followed. The little visit to Philippi was no exception.

Accompanied by Luke the physician, Paul and Silas had sailed to Philippi, a major city and a Roman colony. When the three were on their way to the place of prayer, they came upon a slave girl who was possessed with a demon. This was a horrible situation for the girl, but a boon for her masters, who made quite a profit by sending her out to tell people's fortunes (the ability aided by the demon). The girl decided to follow Paul and his colleagues and taunt them, shouting, "These men are servants of the Most High God, and they have come to tell you how to be saved" (Acts 16:17 NLT). To put it bluntly, the girl was being annoying.

She took to following them day after day, drowning out their voices as they tried to preach, interrupting them as they tried to talk about Jesus, and repeating the same thing over and over. Surely everyone has been in a similar situation. A child keeps asking for candy, saying over and over, "Can I have candy, please please please *please*?" until finally, you snap. And this is just what happened to Paul. But instead of yelling at the girl, he commanded the demon to come out of her.

The masters of the slave girl were furious because their hopes of great fortune were ruined. They dragged Paul and Silas to the authorities and told them that the men were teaching illegal customs. A mob formed quickly against the innocent men, and the city officials beat Paul and Silas severely with wooden rods. As if this wasn't enough punishment for doing nothing wrong, they were then thrown into a dirty prison.

After a few more miraculous events, the "criminals" were set free. The police were forced to apologize to Paul and Silas for publicly beating them without trial and putting them in jail.

Paul got arrested even when he tried to help people. He might have wished for a few more dull moments along the way.

Read the story of Paul and the young girl in Acts 16:16–24.

PART SIX
Momentous Miracles

Rumblin'
and Grumblin'

God Provides Food for Two Million People

PARENTS WHO HAVE LARGE FAMILIES spend a lot of time planning ways to feed everyone. "Let's see. What can we serve a family of six?" When God's people were hungry, there were quite a few mouths to fill, with all the family groups of Israel. In fact, the number of people led by Moses and Aaron was probably around two million.

Two million! Enough to fill a city like Houston. They sprawled across the desert as numerous as the grains of sand.

Now imagine two million voices raised in anger toward their leaders, Moses and Aaron. The cause for their anger? Hunger—two million empty stomachs. So the people rumbled as they grumbled. The popular refrain of the day were words to the effect of, "Why didn't the Lord simply kill us in Egypt? At least we had food there." Yes, life was good in Egypt—apart from the slavery, of course.

Naturally, God got wind of the people's complaints and had a plan. As he told Moses, "Behold, I am about to rain bread from heaven for you, and the people shall go out and gather a day's portion every day, that I may test them, whether they will walk in my law or not" (Exodus 16:4 ESV). Not only that, God planned to provide meat as well. Catered meals!

Well, that was a relief, or was it? The fact that Moses (and later

God) mentioned the people's grumbling proved that their bad attitude was duly noted. The Lord kept his word by sending enough quail to satisfy the hunger. Also, in the morning, the people found frostlike flakes on the ground.

Since they didn't know what the flakes were, they called them *manna,* a Hebrew phrase meaning "What is it?" This was the bread God promised to send from heaven. The only stipulation was that the people were not to leave any of it until the next day. (God had said he would test the people's obedience, remember?) Some people disobeyed, and so found themselves facing maggots and a really bad smell. Moses rebuked them soundly.

On the day before the Sabbath, the people *were* allowed to gather two day's worth of manna without the onslaught of maggots, since no manna would be given on the Sabbath. Nevertheless, some people *still* went out to gather manna on the Sabbath. Another stern rebuke resulted, this time from the Lord. The Sabbath was a day to rest, not a day to do food shopping.

The Bible says that the Israelites miraculously ate manna for forty years. So the people learned to be extremely creative in their manna recipes. Manna was such a significant part of the Israelites' lives that a container of manna was kept in the ark of the covenant. And the Lord continued to send manna until the people arrived at their destination—the Promised Land.

Then it stopped just as suddenly as it had started (see Joshua 5:12).

The stories of the manna and quail can be found in Exodus 16.

The Rock
That Refreshes

God Causes Water to Come from a Rock

THEY'D ONLY BEEN OUT of Egypt a month or so, and it had been no picnic. First, the Hebrews were pursued by their old slave-owners, the Egyptians, and got caught between them and the Red Sea (see "Did You See the Sea?" p. 125). God intervened and saved them, bringing a blanket of water back over the pursuing Egyptians that stopped them cold. Second, the Hebrews discovered that they had no food. God solved that problem too: manna miraculously arrived on the ground every morning (see "Rumblin' and Grumblin'," p. 173).

Third, after marching several days across brittle-dry desert, they found themselves camping at an oasis that had no water. "What did you bring us out here for, Moses?" they cried bitterly. "To die? We could have stayed in Egypt and at least had water to drink. We never lacked that when we were in Egypt."

Moses was at his wit's end. He'd done everything he could do to care for his people, but there was always something else that they clamored for. Now, to be perfectly fair, there *is* nothing quite so desperate as thirst. In what is perhaps the world's driest, thirstiest spot—the Sinai peninsula—these hundreds of thousands of people with their children and cattle were indeed in a world of trouble without water! We can hardly blame them for wanting water and for expecting that someone who led them out into the wilderness must know where to find it. But Moses was at a loss. He kept them moving, a few at a time, toward the next oasis, but he had no real idea of whether there might be enough water for the thousands. As he often did over the next forty years, Moses poured out his miseries before God. "You know," he concluded, "if you don't do something, I think they're getting ready to kill me."

"I'll take care of it," was the comforting reply. The Lord told Moses to lead the people up to a certain rock and to strike it. Water would flow out measureless, bountiful, sweet, refreshing, for all the people and all the animals to drink. He did, and it did, and they did—to their hearts' contentment.

To read more about the water-from-a-rock miracle, see Exodus 17:1–7.

A Donkey's Tale

When a Donkey Talks, Balaam Listens

FAIRY TALES ARE FULL of talking animals, for fairy tales are full of fancy and wonders of the imagination. But everyone knows animals can't really talk, right? That's what Balaam thought too.

During the time when the nation of Israel wandered in the desert toward the Promised Land, other nations noticed them. As the vast people of Israel passed through Moab, the Moabites feared them. Balak, the king of Moab, decided to do something about these interlopers. He sent some officials to a prophet named Balaam with a proposition: "Come and curse the people of Israel." This was not a suggestion to shout expletives at the people; rather, it was a way to have a powerful negative effect on the people of Israel.

While Balaam was not an Israelite, he had some belief in the God of Israel as well as belief in the false gods of the surrounding nations. So Balaam agreed to ask God whether or not he should go with Balak's officials to curse Israel.

The text does not say how Balaam inquired of God, but inquire he did. And God answered: "Do not go with them. You must not put a curse on those people, because they are blessed" (Numbers 22:12 NIV).

The king's officials returned to Balak with Balaam's answer. But Balak was not a man to take no for an answer. More officials with more tempting offers headed to Balaam's home. So back Balaam went before the Lord. This time the Lord allowed Balaam to go with the officials, with the stipulation that Balaam do what the Lord told him to do.

Off Balaam rode on his donkey, little knowing that he had made the Lord angry.

God sent an angel in Balaam's path—a sword-wielding angel—which the donkey was able to see. Being a pretty smart animal, the donkey continually turned aside in the road, trying to avoid that frightening angel and sword. But each time the donkey turned aside, Balaam became angry and beat the donkey, especially when the donkey accidentally jammed Balaam's foot. While this might seem like a slapstick movie, it was a sad reality.

Finally, when the angel moved in front of the donkey, successfully blocking her path, the poor donkey had had enough and simply dropped to the ground. What else was a donkey to do? As Balaam moved to beat the beleaguered donkey yet again, something rather surprising happened. Here's how it went:

The LORD opened the donkey's mouth, and she said to Balaam, "What have I done to you to make you beat me these three times?"

Balaam answered the donkey, "You have made a fool of me! If I had a sword in my hand, I would kill you right now."

The donkey said to Balaam, "Am I not your own donkey, which you have always ridden, to this day? Have I been in the habit of doing this to you?"

"No," he said.

Then the LORD opened Balaam's eyes, and he saw the angel of the LORD standing in the road with his sword drawn. So he bowed low and fell facedown (Numbers 22:28–31).

How interesting that Balaam thought more of his pride than the fact that his donkey talked! Even the angel had words for Balaam concerning his mistreatment of the donkey, saying that the donkey was actually the smarter of the two. He avoided the angel's path three times and thus saved Balaam's life.

A shamefaced Balaam admitted the error of his ways and agreed to return home. The Lord, however, allowed Balaam to continue traveling with Balak's men. But there was no way that Balaam could curse the people God chose to bless. Numbers 23–24 details the messages Balaam gave instead. But it all started with a donkey's tale—one far stranger than any fairy tale.

This extraordinary man-and-his-donkey tale can be found in Numbers 22.

The Longest Day Ever

Joshua's Sun-Stopping Request Ends in Victory for Israel

THE SUMMER SOLSTICE—around June 21—is considered the
longest day of the year. But the longest day ever is recorded in
the Bible. It occurred during the time of Joshua and the conquest of
Canaan. Talk about a land of the "midnight sun"!

After the battle of Ai, which Joshua and the Israelites won after
a second skirmish, five Amorite kings decided to band together to
take on Gibeon. Why Gibeon? Because the people of this city made
a treaty with Israel (see "Gulled by the Gibeonites," p. 90). These
kings lived nearby in Jerusalem, Hebron, Lachish, Eglon, and Jar-
muth. Gibeon was strategically located and had a great fighting
force. Yet they surrendered to Israel! So the five kings wanted revenge against Gibeon for daring to side with Israel.

Well, the Gibeonites turned to their new allies, the Israelites,
for help. Joshua was obligated to bring the army along for a skirmish, and God gave him the assurance of victory.

Joshua and his men marched all night and attacked right away
on the following morning—an amazing display of endurance. But
they didn't fight alone. God was with them, sending hailstones hur-
tling upon the enemy forces, which took out more of the enemy
than Joshua's troops did.

The enemy soldiers were confused and terrified . . . the common response when the Lord aided the people of Israel. While in
pursuit of the fleeing soldiers, Joshua made a strange request of
the Lord: "Let the sun stand still over Gibeon, and the moon over

the valley of Aijalon" (Joshua 10:12 NLT). He wanted to finish the battle once and for all, rather than letting it drag on another day.

God agreed to the request and allowed the sun to stop and not go down for a full day. While this phenomenon might not seem strange to those who have seen the sun at midnight around the Arctic Circle, it was definitely abnormal at this time and this place.

The five kings ran for their lives and hid in a cave near a town called Makkedah. But they couldn't hide for long. After having the mouth of the cave blocked, Joshua and his troops continued pursuing the enemies. When all were defeated, Joshua and his men returned to the cave.

The five kings, who were probably nervous wrecks by then, were brought out. Joshua gave the army of Israel a pep talk, explaining what God would do to the enemies of Israel. He then demonstrated by having his commanders place their feet on the necks of the kings—a way to humiliate the enemy. Afterward, each king was killed.

Then the sun was allowed to set, thus ending a very long day.

To get the full story on this delayed day, read Joshua 10:1–28.

Special Delivery

God Uses Ravens to Bring Food to His Prophet

BIRDS CAN BE TRAINED to do many things. They can carry messages and hunt on command. Seldom do we read of birds delivering food to creatures other than baby birds. Yet God used ravens in a heavenly food-delivery service to a hungry prophet. It all began with a drought.

During the time of Moses, God made a covenant with Israel. He would be faithful to them if they were faithful to him. They would be blessed and would avoid horrible curses, like famine and the deaths of livestock, if they kept their agreement with God (see Deuteronomy 28). Unfortunately, a series of kings who made bad decisions inspired the people of Israel to worship false gods.

Ahab was one of the bad kings. If there were a contest to determine which king was the worst, Ahab would be one of the top contenders. He solidified his chances of winning "Worst King Ever" by marrying Jezebel—a Sidonian princess who worshiped Baal and Asherah. Ahab joined his wife in her worship by setting up an altar to Baal in the temple. Perhaps this action scored points with Jezebel, but it infuriated God.

God chose Elijah, a man from the town of Tishbe, to be his spokesperson before Ahab. Elijah's message was simple: "There will be neither dew nor rain in the next few years except at my word" (1 Kings 17:1 NIV).

Why a drought? Baal was considered the god of rain clouds and fertility. As with the gods of Egypt during the time of Moses, God wanted to send a message that only the true God can control the elements.

With the loss of rain came a famine that affected the obedient and the disobedient. But God was not about to let his man go hungry. He sent Elijah to a brook east of the Jordan River. There he arranged for an unusual catering service. God explained, "You shall drink of the brook, and I have commanded the ravens to feed you there" (1 Kings 17:4 AMP).

In literature ravens often are the bad guys—the harbingers of death in poems such as "The Raven" by Edgar Allan Poe, or part of the evil ambience of Saruman in Tolkien's *Lord of the Rings* trilogy. But this time, God used them to be the heroes. Morning and evening, a rotation of ravens delivered meat and bread to Elijah. Amazing!

Elijah's story showed that God not only had the power to stop the rain, but he also had the compassion and faithfulness to provide for his people.

Elijah's special-delivery story can be found in 1 Kings 17:1–6.

KINGS AND PROPHETS CHRONOLOGY

PROPHET	KING[S] SERVED
Samuel	Saul; David
Nathan	David; Solomon
Ahijah	Jeroboam I of Israel
Elijah	Ahab of Israel
Micaiah	Ahab of Israel; Jehoshaphat of Judah
Jehu	Jehoshaphat of Judah
Obadiah	Jehoram of Judah
Elisha	Joram, Jehu, Jehoahaz, and Jehoash of Israel
Joel	Joash of Judah
Jonah	Jeroboam II of Israel; the Assyrians

PROPHET	KING[S] SERVED
Amos	Jeroboam II of Israel
Hosea	Jeroboam II, Zechariah, Shallum, Menahem, Pekahiah, Pekah, and Hoshea of Israel; Azariah (Uzziah), Jotham, Ahaz, and Hezekiah of Judah
Micah	Jotham, Ahaz, and Hezekiah of Judah
Isaiah	Azariah (Uzziah), Jotham, Ahaz, Hezekiah, and Manasseh of Judah
Nahum	Manasseh of Judah
Zephaniah	Josiah of Judah
Jeremiah	Josiah, Jehoahaz, Jehoiakim, Jehoiachin, and Zedekiah of Judah
Habakkuk	Josiah, Jehoahaz, Jehoiakim, Jehoiachin, and Zedekiah of Judah
Daniel	Nebuchadnezzar and Belshazzar of Babylon; Darius and Cyrus of Persia
Ezekiel	The people in exile in Babylon during the reign of Nebuchadnezzar

The Crisco
Keeps Coming

A Widow Reaps a Wealth of Oil

IF YOU COULD HAVE an unlimited supply of anything (besides money), what would you ask for? Patience? Food? Gas for your car? Would you want all the Crisco oil you could get? Well, that's what a widow received when she asked Elisha for help.

A woman in Bible times had no source of income if she didn't have a husband or sons. The land of Palestine had a plethora of poor widows. This particular widow had sons, but when a creditor threatened to take them as slaves, she faced a real disaster. Who was she going to call? Certainly not "ghostbusters." Being the widow of a prophet, she knew the right man with the right plan: the prophet Elisha.

Elisha was the successor of Elijah (the prophet of Mount Carmel fame; see "Duel on Mount Carmel," p. 49) and the man who asked for a double portion of Elijah's power (see 2 Kings 2:9). God, always pleased with bold faith, agreed to his request. Consequently, Elisha had the reputation of performing great wonders through the power of God.

Once the widow explained her problem, Elisha came up with a practical solution. The widow was to collect all the jars she could find.

What would you have done if you were told to do this? Once

you stopped laughing, perhaps you would have called in someone to deal with the "crackpot." But the widow didn't laugh. Instead, she borrowed jars and miraculously kept filling them with oil. The oil continued to flow until there was not one jar left that *hadn't* been filled with oil. This is the kind of miracle Jesus would later perform (see John 2).

What's great about this story is the widow's faith in the power of God as shown through Elisha. Obviously she didn't borrow just one jar and call it a day. She kept borrowing jars until there were no more jars left in the area to borrow. She had enough oil to pay the creditors and save her sons from a life of slavery. They also had enough money to live on.

Perhaps the widow could relate to these thankful words of David: "My cup overflows" (Psalm 23:5 NIV).

The widow's request can be found in 2 Kings 4:1–7.

A Son Also Rises

Elisha Raises a Widow's Dead Son to Life

DEATH IS usually viewed as "the final frontier," the period at the end of a sentence. But if you were around during the days of Elisha, you might have seen the dead walk.

Dateline: Shunem—the home of an unnamed wealthy woman who is about to find herself in the twilight zone of despair. But first, we see her offering her home and food to a prophet known as Elisha.

In Bible times, there were few roadside inns and no four-star hotels. Travelers depended on the hospitality of others. Knowing of Elisha's itinerant ministry, the woman gave him *carte blanche* to stay with her and her husband, and she threw in groceries too.

Wishing to reward her for her kindness, Elisha asked his servant Gehazi what she would like. When Gehazi replied that she was childless, Elisha declared that she would have a son in the following year.

All's well that ends well, right? Wrong. Years later, the child suddenly dropped dead due to a mysterious head ailment and only managed to make it to his father before dying. Now you might wonder, *What sort of a reward is this? Her child's dead!* But death was not the end of the story. The woman decided to seek out Elisha for help.

Knowing how distressed she was, Elisha didn't bother with pithy "there, there" statements. Instead, he handed his staff to Gehazi and told him to lay it on the child. And no dawdling on the way, Gehazi! Even though Gehazi ran like the wind and followed Elisha's instructions to the letter, nothing happened.

There are some jobs you just have to do yourself. So Elisha went to the woman's house and, after praying, placed himself on the child. His mentor, Elijah, when faced with raising the son of a widow to life, had done the same thing (see 1 Kings 17:17–24). But with Elisha, *nothing happened!* The child was still lifeless.

Well, Elisha wasn't a miracle-working prophet for nothing. Instead of giving up or pouting, Elisha stretched out on the child again. Finally, the boy began to sneeze. He was alive!

The miracles God allows are not always instantaneous. Case in point: Jesus caused a blind man to see after spitting on him and laying hands on him. But the man didn't see correctly the first time Jesus touched him (see "The Ol' Spit and Polish," p. 232). And if you know anything about Elijah's raising-the-dead-to-life story, you know that he had to perform the same action three times.

Sometimes God allows faith to be tested through the delays. But stories like this remind us that God has the final say, even over death.

Read this amazing life-and-death saga in 2 Kings 4:8–37.

A Prophet Picks
a Peck of Poison

Elisha Solves a Poison Problem with Just the Right Ingredient

EVER READ A MYSTERY where someone is poisoned to death? Many times, the poisoner is someone being blackmailed or even someone who hopes to gain an inheritance by bumping off the victim. Or sometimes, the butler *did* do it! But you've probably never read a mystery involving a helpful prophet who poisons a group of people by accident. But that's what happened during a time of famine in Elisha's day.

Although he often traveled alone or with his servant Gehazi, Elisha sometimes had dealings with other prophets in the area. He met with them and ate with them. During one of those meetings, when the suggestion was made to put on a pot of stew, one of Elisha's servants went out and found some herbs and some wild gourds to add to the pot.

If you've taken a class in wilderness survival, perhaps you've drawn a shocked breath at this point and are frantically wondering if the man knew what he was getting himself into. We may never know what the man thought, other than something like, *Mmmm. This will add some flavor to that savory stew!* But the fact remains that the gourds he brought back with him (and that plant was not named in the Bible) were added to the pot.

The prophets couldn't wait to dig in. After all, who knew how many meals they might have missed, what with the famine and all. But someone eventually discovered that the first bite of stew could possibly have been the last thing any of them ever ate. The stew had been poisoned!

Lest you think the prophet and his servant were ancient versions of "Arsenic Annie" (who poisoned eleven people in 1927 with poisoned prunes), consider the fact that no one actually died . . . yet. But the stew *was* inedible. (Really rotten luck during a famine.)

Before anyone could say, "The butler did it," Elisha went into action. Now Elisha never claimed to be Betty Crocker or Rachael Ray. But he knew just the right ingredient to throw into the pot of poisoned stew: flour. Once flour was added, the stew became good enough to eat. Just don't try this at home with oleander and Gold Medal flour!

Read all about this "potboiler" in 2 Kings 4:38–41.

Weird and Wonderful Foods in the Bible

Curious about the culinary delights experienced during Bible times? Interested in locusts de jour or manna marinara? Many people in Bible times would say yes! Here are just a few of the interesting foods or beverages mentioned in the Bible.

Food	Reference	Reason for It
Fruit from the tree of the knowledge of good and evil	Genesis 2:9–17; 3:1–24	The Bible is not specific about the kind of fruit on this tree. But God banned Adam and Eve from eating it. When they ate from it, the world was changed.
Manna and quail	Exodus 16	These "fine flakes, as fine as frost on the ground" (Exodus 16:14 HCSB) were given the name *manna* which is Hebrew for "what is it?" This was the way God provided for his people during their wilderness wanderings.
Water mixed with gold powder	Exodus 32:19–20	When the Israelites made a golden calf, an angry Moses burned the calf, ground the remains, and flung them into water. He then forced the people to drink the water.
Honey from a lion's carcass	Judges 14:8–9	Samson killed a lion and left it on the road. When he returned later, he discovered that a swarm of bees had taken it over and made honey within it. He ate some of the honey and took some to his parents (but didn't tell them where he got it!).
Poisoned stew	2 Kings 4:38–41	A prophet inadvertently served poisoned herb stew to a company of prophets. But Elisha was on hand to perform a miracle that made the stew edible.

Food	Reference	Reason for It
Tears	Psalm 42:3	In moments of sorrow, David had all he could eat.
A scroll	Ezekiel 3:1–3	Ezekiel was told to eat a scroll—a message to God's people. Although God's words were sweet, the message of God's judgment would be difficult.
Locusts and wild honey	Matthew 3:4	The foods of choice for John the Baptist
Jesus' body and blood	Matthew 26:26–29; John 6:22–59; 1 Corinthians 11:17–34	Jesus' body and blood, represented in the Eucharist, symbolize the need for a believer to associate with the death of Christ.
A scroll	Revelation 10:9–11	An angel told John to eat a scroll—a message of suffering.

Munchies for Many

Elisha Takes Loaves and Feeds More Than a Hundred People

I N BIBLE TIMES, prophets were the celebrities of their day. Everyone knew who they were, which was not always good, especially if a crowd of people hated what the prophet had to say and knew where he lived. But in this case it was a good thing.

If you read "A Prophet Picks a Peck of Poison" (p. 187), you know that the prophet Elisha lived through a time of famine. His mentor, Elijah, also suffered through a famine in his day (see 1 Kings 17). When we're hungry, we might think, *I'm starving*, but most of us have never faced real starvation. Famines were a judgment of God on a people determined to disobey him by worshiping idols. Consider the fact that God was in the habit of providing food like manna to feed his hungry people during their travels in the wilderness or rain to help the plants grow. He promised to continue doing that if they obeyed him (see Deuteronomy 28). When the people rejected God, they suffered consequences like famines. But famines affected everyone—the good and the bad.

As with Elijah, God miraculously provided for Elisha and the people of Israel by prompting a man to bring twenty loaves of bread to Elisha. Perhaps the man gave the bread as a way of supporting the prophet, the way a person would contribute to the upkeep of a priest or king. And bread was a staple in Bible times. Sometimes the poor had only bread to eat. But when Elisha generously suggested, "Give it to the people to eat" (2 Kings 4:42 NIV), the bread giver probably looked at him dubiously. Hello? How could twenty loaves (and these might have been small loaves) feed a hundred people?

Are you getting the Jesus-feeding-the-five-thousand vibe yet? Just wait.

Elisha didn't break a sweat, wring his hands, or tell the man to "Let them eat cake," Marie Antoinette style. He knew the kind of God he served—big, powerful, able to do anything. He knew that God could somehow multiply the bread to feed the crowd. And that's what happened. Everyone had bread to eat. There were even leftovers!

Once again, Elisha foreshadowed the kind of ministry Jesus

would have someday—one that went beyond just the pat-on-the-back, go-in-peace blessing and all the way to the miraculous.

It was a good thing.

Elisha's bread story can be found in 2 Kings 4:42–44.

A Slam Dunk

Several Dips in the Jordan River Result in Healing

THERE ARE MANY beautiful lakes and rivers in the world. The Jordan River is not considered one of them. In Bible times it was known for being muddy. But it has the reputation of being a sacred river, and it was sometimes the site of the miraculous.

During the time of the great prophet Elisha, the protégé of Elijah, there lived a man named Naaman. Naaman distinguished himself as a commander of the Aramean (Syrian) army. Life was good for Naaman and probably would have seemed perfect had it not been for one small problem—he had leprosy (known as Hansen's disease today). Leprosy was a terrible skin disease that sometimes led to the loss of limbs. It was a slow death sentence.

A captive servant girl from Israel told Naaman's wife that Naaman should seek the prophet in Samaria to find a cure. But the people of Israel and Aram didn't often get along, as evidenced by the fact that Naaman's servant girl had been taken from her homeland and forced into slavery. However, this unnamed girl kindly tried to help her master regain his health.

Naaman was well liked by the king, who readily gave his permission for Naaman to travel to Israel. He even supplied a letter to the king of Israel and gave Naaman a generous expense account as well. Unfortunately, the king of Israel (Joram) had no idea why he received such a letter, especially since in it he was told to cure Naaman!

Thankfully, Elisha learned of the letter and told the king that Naaman needed to drop by his house. So Naaman headed there in all of his pomp and splendor. Imagine Naaman's surprise when, instead of talking directly to Naaman, Elisha talked through a messenger! Not only that, Elisha's only piece of advice was for Naaman to go and wash in the muddy Jordan River seven times! A double insult! Surely there were better rivers to use!

But Naaman's servants talked him out of simply going away angry. What would it hurt for him to take the prophet's advice?

So off to the Jordan River went Naaman and his entourage. Naaman dipped in the Jordan, probably feeling foolish each time. But seven dips later, he was completely healed! And he realized something he hadn't realized before: there was a God in Israel.

To read more about Naaman's river dipping, read 2 Kings 5:1–19.

Ax on the Water

A Borrowed Ax Head Does the Impossible

WITH OUR SADLY POLLUTED lakes and rivers, perhaps we're not shocked at what we've seen floating about. But an iron ax head will always be an uncommon sight on top of a river.

The Jordan River was never the cleanest river in Palestine. If you read "A Slam Dunk" (p. 192), you know that Naaman, the Aramean army commander, had no desire to wade through its muck. But doing so changed his life. Once again, God would use the prophet Elisha to cause the miraculous to come to pass at the Jordan.

A group of prophets decided to build a meeting place near the Jordan River. As with any do-it-yourself project, tools were needed. And since there were no Ace Hardware or Lowe's Home Improvement stores back in that day, tools had to be borrowed. The tool of choice was an ax—perfect for felling trees in the days before the advent of chain saws.

As is generally the case with borrowed things—especially expensive borrowed things—something went wrong. While a tree was in the process of being cut, the heavy iron ax head fell off and into the Jordan. According to the laws of physics, objects with higher density than the liquid in which they are immersed will sink. Archimedes, the ancient Greek mathematician and physicist, developed a fancy formula for determining an object's density in relation to the surrounding fluid:

$$\text{Relative density} = \frac{\text{Weight}}{\text{Weight} - \text{Immersed weight}}$$

So that ax head was gone for good . . . or so they thought. This was a disaster not only for the building project but for the person who borrowed the ax head. Replacing it would have been next to impossible.

But Elisha happened to be on the scene. When he was told about the dilemma, he didn't immediately think of buoyancy, the density of the ax head, or Archimedes. Instead, he thought of God, the Creator, who made everything that mathematicians and physicists theorized about. Elisha's solution: toss a stick in the water.

How on earth will that solve anything? we might wonder at this point. Apparently, it did. The ax head floated to the top of the water as if it were as light as smoke. God once again proved that not only could he change the laws of physics, but he could also change a bad situation into something good for those who trusted him.

You can find the ax still floating in 2 Kings 6:1–7.

Storm Stopper

When Jesus Says, "Stop," a Storm Stills

THE FURY OF A STORM frightens most people. News stories are full of the devastation caused by hurricanes, tropical storms, nor'easters, and microbursts. Even some rain storms can cause enough flooding to wreak havoc in an area.

Imagine being out in a boat in the middle of a squall. There's something about being out in the middle of a big expanse of water in a small boat with waves crashing that makes you feel extra vulnerable. That was how the fishing crew of the *Andrea Gail* felt in *The Perfect Storm*, the 1997 book by Sebastian Junger, which detailed the disastrous 1991 storm. That was also how Jesus' disciples felt almost two thousand years ago in a little storm of their own.

One day, after a hard day of preaching and teaching, Jesus climbed into a boat with his disciples to cross the Sea of Galilee. The Sea of Galilee, which was really a lake, was known for sudden storms, and this day confirmed that reputation.

Picture it: dark sky, rain-heavy clouds, waves pounding the boat. This was a recipe for disaster. The disciples were terrified.

Keep in mind that many of the disciples were experienced fishermen who sailed often on this lake. If *they* were afraid, this storm had to be a doozy. Perhaps it was the "perfect storm"—one formed under just the right conditions; for example, low-pressure warm air meeting a high-pressure cold front.

Okay, picture this now: dark sky, rain-heavy clouds, waves pounding the boat, sleeping Savior. Which item doesn't seem to match the others? The disciples picked the last item. After frantically waking Jesus, they complained, "Teacher, don't you care if we drown?" (Mark 4:38 NIV).

Jesus jumped up and said, "Quiet! Be still!" (Mark 4:39). But he wasn't talking to the complaining disciples. He was talking to the wind and the boat-swamping waves.

Have you ever heard anyone scream "Be still" in the middle of a storm, especially one devastating enough to take lives? The disciples probably never heard such a thing either. But the words from Jesus' mouth had an immediate effect. The wind stopped. The waves ceased pounding.

With that calamity over with, Jesus brought up the disciples' lack of faith.

There's something about being in the middle of a lake in a small

boat with a Savior who just calmed a squall that causes intense vulnerability. Even though they were safe, the disciples were *still* terrified. After witnessing such an amazing display of mastery over a
storm, they couldn't fathom what Jesus was all about. How could a
mere man still a storm? A mere man could not. But a God-man could.
*You can read about the storm stilled by Jesus in Matthew 8:23–27; Mark 4:35–41;
and Luke 8:22–25.*

Stretching a Meal

*Jesus Makes a Boy's Lunch Stretch to Feed More Than Five
Thousand People*

IF YOU HAVE A FAMILY or are living on a budget, you know
what it's like to stretch a meal—to feed a number of people as
economically as possible. That's why foods such as rice and bread are
staples. In Bible times, bread was the prime food that most people
could afford. Sometimes, it was the only food people had.

During the days when Jesus walked the earth, food was not as
close as the nearest refrigerator or grocery store. So imagine the
magnitude of the situation when thousands of people followed Jesus
to an area out in the middle of nowhere. They eagerly brought
friends and loved ones who were sick, because they knew that Jesus
was a miracle worker.

The practical-minded disciples quickly realized that the people would grow hungry soon. They decided that maybe it was time for Jesus to wrap things up by giving the benediction and sending the crowd away to forage for food.

Instead, Jesus asked one of the disciples (Philip), "Where are we to buy bread, so that all these people may eat?" (John 6:5 AMP). Like any good teacher, Jesus asked his students questions to test their knowledge. Imagine having a pop quiz like that! How would you answer, especially after hearing Jesus say, "Give them something to eat yourselves" (Mark 6:37 AMP)? Perhaps Jesus knew that Philip was mathematically inclined, because Philip immediately calculated how much it would cost to feed the crowd—more than eight months' wages.

Andrew, the brother of Peter, was even more practical. Somehow, he found a kid with five barley loaves and two fish. But even Andrew was stumped about how to stretch this small meal so far. After all, there were over five thousand people present. More than likely the actual number was double that, since wives and children were not usually counted.

Jesus had a plan in mind for feeding the people. Remember, this is the same person who calmed a storm (see "Storm Stopper," p. 195). First, the people needed to be organized into groups. With that done, he took the boy's lunch, thanked God the Father for it, then started handing the food out. Group 1: here you go. Group 2: here's some for you . . . and on and on.

Perhaps the people in the back row were sweating at this point. Would the bread and fish last? Would only the people up front get to eat? Would a riot start if the food ran out?

But Jesus continued to hand out bread and fish. Who knows how long he stood there handing it to the disciples to distribute to the people. Hours, undoubtedly. But the fact remains that every person there was given food.

If you read "Munchies for Many" (p. 190), you read the story of Elisha's miraculous feeding of one hundred people. Here was a crowd probably a hundred times that amount—and there were twelve baskets full of leftovers! Did you get that? *Twelve baskets.* And how many disciples were there? Twelve! Perhaps those baskets served as a reminder to them that when it came to stretching food— and stretching faith—Jesus was the Master.

Other than the Resurrection, this amazing meal is the only miracle recorded in all four Gospels. You can find it in Matthew 14:13–21; Mark 6:30–44; Luke 9:10–17; and John 6:1–15.

Wade on the Water

Jesus Walks on Water

THIS HAS TO BE one of the best publicized of Jesus' miraculous acts. Walking on water has become a universal representation of the impossible, the miraculous, the supernatural. Even today, among biblically illiterate people, we often hear expressions like, "Yeah, he can do everything but walk on water," spoken of a popular sports figure or a political candidate who has an enthusiastic following. The ability to walk on water appears to be some sort of tacitly understood borderline between the miraculous and the merely astonishing. Chinese and French acrobats perform astounding physical feats; young Asian children solve extraordinary mathematical problems; old, wrinkled African storytellers and archive keepers recite ancient records and genealogies flawlessly for hours at a time. But nobody, no one, walks on water.

So on that dark, stormy night when the twelve disciples in a light boat struggling against a head-on wind saw a figure walking across the choppy waves, they were frightened out of their wits.

"It's a ghost," someone yelled, and they all instantly agreed that it was, indeed, and the fear they already felt in the mounting waves and stormy weather clicked up a notch—to panic. Hey, wouldn't we react the same way, to see a human figure walking above the water in the middle of the night? Their reaction is completely natural. But Jesus quickly spoke and told them it was he and that they should not fear.

Matthew adds the strange but completely in-character response of Peter: "Lord, if it is you, command me to come to you on the water" (Matthew 14:28 NRSV). Only Peter would say such a thing, and only Peter would actually do it.

Jesus said, "Come on, then," and Peter was as good as his (impulsive) word. He actually climbed out of the boat, stepped on top of the water, and started making his way toward Jesus on the top of the waves. It only lasted a few seconds, but it was enough to get him within a few feet of Jesus. He got that far before he looked around at the howling wind and the waves surging up beside him, and he suddenly realized he didn't belong out there. At that moment, he began to slide down into the water.

As soon as he called out to Jesus, the latter reached out, grabbed him, and pulled him into the boat with him, saying, "Why'd you doubt? You were doing great there for a while."

Jesus' arrival in the boat signaled the end of the black storm too. As he and Peter settled into the boat, the sea became calm and the sky cleared, so the disciples could see that only a few stars were left still burning and light was coming up in the east.

A new day with new possibilities.

To read more about this amazing story, see Matthew 14:22–33; Mark 6:45–52; and John 6:16–21.

TRAVELING BY SEA

In the days before airplanes, traveling by sea was the only way to get to a far-off shore or even one close by.

SEA VOYAGER[S]	DESTINATION
Jonah	While trying to escape from God's command to go to Nineveh, Jonah jumped aboard a ship heading for Tarshish—in the opposite direction across the Mediterranean Sea. God sent a storm that nearly wrecked the ship. Jonah wound up overboard and was soon swallowed by a huge fish. Jonah continued his sea voyage in the fish's stomach (Jonah 1–2).
Jesus and his disciples	While Jesus and his disciples traveled in a boat on the Sea of Galilee, a storm struck. But Jesus calmed it (Matthew 8:23–27; Mark 4:35–41; Luke 8:22–25).
Jesus (and probably his disciples)	Jesus traveled by boat across the Sea of Galilee from the region of the Gadarenes to Capernaum in Galilee. There he healed a paralyzed man (Matthew 9:1–9; Mark 2:1–12; Luke 5:17–26).
Jesus' disciples	After feeding over five thousand people, Jesus sent his disciples aboard a boat that sailed across the Sea of Galilee. Jesus met them by walking on the water (Matthew 14:22–33; Mark 6:45–52; John 6:16–21).
Jesus, Peter, James, and John	While preaching, Jesus found himself pushed to the edge of the Sea of Galilee (Lake of Gennesaret). He climbed into Peter's boat and told Peter to sail to deeper waters. There Peter made a miraculous catch of fish. After calling his partners—James and John, the sons of Zebedee—to help, Peter realized that he was in the presence of someone holy. Peter, James, and John left everything to follow Jesus (Luke 5:1–11).

SEA VOYAGER[S]	DESTINATION
Paul and Barnabas	After being called by the Holy Spirit, Paul and Barnabas set sail from Seleucia to Cyprus, where they preached in synagogues. They later sailed from Paphos to Perga. It was here that John Mark (writer of the Gospel of Mark) left the company (Acts 13:1–13). Paul, Barnabas, and others in the missionary entourage traveled to Pisidian Antioch and preached in the synagogue there. At the end of the ministry on this first missionary journey, they sailed from Attalia back to Antioch (Acts 14:26).
Paul, Silas, and others	After a disagreement with Barnabas (Acts 15:36–40), Paul traveled with other missionaries, including Silas and Luke, the author of Acts (note his use of the pronoun "we"). He set out with Silas to Derbe. At this point, Paul learned through a dream that he was called to Macedonia. This involved another boat trip. They left from Troas and landed first at Samothrace, then went on to Neapolis, the port of Philippi. The Roman colony of Philippi was the ultimate destination. After land travels through Greece to Corinth, Paul returned across the sea first to Ephesus and then back to Jerusalem (Acts 16:1–18:22).
Paul, Luke, and others	Just as he planned to go to Syria, Paul learned that some Jews plotted to take his life. He decided to return to Macedonia and sailed from Philippi to Troas (Acts 20:1–6).

SEA VOYAGER[S]	DESTINATION
Paul	After being in Troas for a time, Paul decided to return to Jerusalem at the bidding of the Holy Spirit. He sailed from Assos to Mitylene to Kios, then on to Samos, and finally arrived at Miletus (Acts 20). After meeting with the Ephesian church leaders, Paul and company sailed to Cos, then moved on to Rhodes and Patara before switching ships. They continued on to Tyre, where Paul was warned not to go to Jerusalem. He decided to go anyway. The ship then landed at Ptolemais. After a day, they arrived at Caesarea (Acts 21).
Paul, Priscilla, and Aquila	After a haircut, Paul sailed for Syria with Priscilla and Aquila, but he left them in Ephesus, where he reasoned with the Jews (Acts 18:18–21).
Paul	En route to stand trial in Rome, Paul set sail at Adramyttium (a harbor east of Assos) and experienced difficulties in Fair Havens. Paul was all for waiting out the winter, but the centurion accompanying Paul decided to ignore his advice. While sailing along Crete, a storm struck, leaving them shipwrecked on the island of Malta (Acts 27:1–28:10). After leaving Malta, they sailed in an Alexandrian ship to Syracuse, Rhegium, and then to Puteoli (Acts 28:11–15).

Lunchables
and Leftovers

Jesus Provides a Meal for Four Thousand People

EVER BEEN IN A REMOTE PLACE where food wasn't readily available? When hiking or camping or on a "walkabout," you have to bring your own food along, unless you know how to forage out in the wild.

Jesus was no stranger to remote locations. Having no earthly home of his own, he traveled about doing the tasks he was sent to do: healing the sick, preaching about the kingdom of God. Often crowds—thousands of people—followed him to out-of-the-way places, hoping to gain a minute of his time—knowing that he wouldn't turned anyone away. That was the plight of a popular speaker/teacher/miracle worker.

Jesus was all three of these things, and he was also very practical. After three days of crowds following him around, he noticed that the people were probably hungry. But they couldn't just head to the convenience store for some ramen noodles or Oscar Mayer/Kraft Lunchables. Remember the remote location. Perhaps the crowds had to travel some distance and several hours to get to it. The practical Savior knew that many would probably faint from hunger if they tried to make it back to the nearest town to find food.

What to do? What to do? The disciples weren't sure. (Who

knows if they recalled the meal Jesus provided for more than five thousand (see "Stretching a Meal," p. 197). Although they collected seven loaves and a few fish, they couldn't fathom how these items could feed a crowd that numbered over four thousand (excluding women and children). They could do the math. There wasn't enough bread or fish to provide even a crumb for each person.

But Jesus took the bread and fish—the ancient form of the Lunchable—and gave thanks. Then he got to work, doling them out to groups of people. The disciples didn't just stand there watching and wondering, *Wow. How's he doing that?* They were put to work in the distribution side of this enterprise. But did they hand out crumbs? Nope. Everyone ate bread and fish. "They all ate as much as they wanted" (Matthew 15:37 NLT). Amazing! But what was even more amazing was that there were leftovers! No one expected a doggie bag with this meal. Yet the disciples collected seven baskets of leftovers.

The baskets of broken bread and fish were proof of who Jesus was: the Savior who could do anything. He was the "bread from heaven" (John 6:32 NIV) who would one day be broken for them.

This remarkable bread and fish meal is recorded in Matthew 15:32–39 and Mark 8:1–10.

Shine, Jesus, Shine

The Disciples Are Bathed in Son Light When Jesus Is Transfigured

N O ONE in his right mind would stare directly into the sun for a long time. You'd go blind if you did—burn those retinas clean away. But three of Jesus' disciples found themselves staring directly at the shining glory of the "Son." Instead of going blind, they came away changed.

Although he had twelve disciples, Jesus seemed closest to three: Peter, James, and John. They were with him when he performed astounding feats. One of the most astounding things they witnessed was not so much about what Jesus did (feed five thousand; bring the dead back to life), but who Jesus was—his real essence.

Jesus brought the three men to a mountain. In many Bible stories, mountains were the scenes of amazing encounters with God. God told Abraham to take his son Isaac and slay him on Mount Moriah but spared him at the last second (see Genesis 22). God gave Moses the Ten Commandments on Mount Sinai (see Exodus 19–20). God proved himself to be the only true God when Elijah called down fire on Mount Carmel (see 1 Kings 18). God whispered to the weary prophet Elijah at Mount Horeb (see 1 Kings 19). Now, Jesus' disciples were about to have another close encounter of the amazing kind.

When we look at our best friend, what do we see? Someone we love, undoubtedly, but someone pretty ordinary, right? Peter, James, and John had looked at their best friend day after day. They saw a man who grew weary, ate food, and put on his cloak like anyone else. But up on the mountain that day, they saw something out of the ordinary when Jesus transformed before their very eyes. Jesus showed his side that the disciples didn't normally see—his glory. His face shone like the sun, and his clothes blazed with white light. Incredible!

As if that weren't amazing enough, two other men appeared with Jesus: Moses and Elijah. Yes, *the* Moses and Elijah, the representatives of the Law and the prophets. Whoa! Just imagine people you admired from the past—who lived thousands of years ago—suddenly popping up before you. What would you say? What would you do?

The disciples were undoubtedly stunned senseless. Peter's words sound like those of a man trying to grasp at the ungraspable: "If you want, I'll make three shelters as memorials—one for you, one for Moses, and one for Elijah" (Matthew 17:4 NLT).

But there was more to come. An unusual cloud appeared, and the disciples heard a voice speak from it. It was God, giving his seal of approval to his Son: "This is my dearly loved Son, who brings me great joy. Listen to him" (Matthew 17:5). God had only spoken like that one other time—when Jesus was baptized (see Matthew 3:17).

That did it! The disciples fell to the ground scared out of their wits—the usual posture of those who truly see or hear from God or a representative sent by him. (See, for example, Daniel 10:7–9; Revelation 1:17.) But Jesus had compassion on them and calmed their fear. When they were ready to finally get off the ground, they realized that only Jesus remained, looking as he normally did—like the Son of God who dimmed his glory, just for a little while, to walk among men.

Jesus' glorious transformation is recorded in Matthew 17:1–13 and Mark 9:2–13.

Fish Finances

Peter Pays the Temple Tax in a Fishy Way

WHAT A COMBINATION of genres this story is: whopper fish story, get-the-best-of-the-taxman anecdote, and demonstration of Jesus' divine sovereignty over the created world, all rolled into one! Moreover, in this story Jesus' whimsical or humorous side appears, which is a welcome window on an aspect of his personality that is not often featured in the books and movies about his life. Here's how it played out.

Peter was put between a rock and hard place by the temple-tax collectors, who asked him menacingly, "Doesn't your teacher pay the temple tax?" (Matthew 17:24 NIV).

A bit intimidated, Peter blurted out, "Certainly he does!" Then he had second thoughts as he scurried away, turning the matter over in his mind. *I wonder . . . maybe he doesn't. I hadn't thought about that until now. But now I've opened my big mouth and said that he does pay it. What if it's a matter of principle for him not to pay it?* He arrived back at his house in a state of uncertainty and doubt, and there was Jesus himself.

Jesus, knowing what had transpired, perhaps had a little fun with Peter before solving the problem. "So, Peter, what do you think? Just hypothetically speaking, of course. Do kings of the earth charge taxes to their children or to others?"

Peter: "To others."

Jesus: "So that means that the children are free, right? We who are the children of God should not have to pay taxes on our Father's house, then, should we? Eh, Peter?"

Peter was squirming and turning red in the face, wondering how he was going to explain what he had told the tax collectors, when Jesus said, "Okay, here's what we'll do. Peter, you go fishing. You're good at it. But we don't need a whole netful this time. Just take your pole and line, throw the hook in, and the first fish you catch is all we need. When you open his mouth, you'll find a coin in it, which is worth exactly twice the temple tax. Take that coin back to the folks who stopped you on the street, and give them the coin. Tell them it's for you and for me."

Peter rushed out of the room to do his master's bidding, and Jesus must have chuckled for several minutes afterward.

It would be nice if all tax transactions were that uncomplicated.

To read this fish-and-coin story, see Matthew 17:24–27.

One Strike
and It's Out!

Jesus Heals a Demon-Possessed Man on the Sabbath

JESUS HAD little patience with demons. With fallen, redeemable people, yes; that was a different story. But fallen angels were on a one-way trip to condemnation. They had rebelled against God and his purposes, and there was no turning back for them.

Demons are real—make no mistake about it. The Bible describes them as fallen angels who joined Satan in his rebellion against God. As evil spirits under Satan's control, they prowl around and try to make trouble for people. At times, even "demon possession" occurs, whereby a person is under the control of an evil spirit. That's what had occurred for the unfortunate man in this story.

Jesus was in Capernaum and went to the synagogue on the Sabbath. He began to teach, amazing everyone with his authority. And on this day, even an evil spirit was impressed. A man (possessed by an evil spirit) in the synagogue suddenly began screaming out, "I know who you really are, 'Jesus of Nazareth.' What are you going to do, O Holy One? Destroy us? Throw us into the abyss? It's not time yet, you know."

Jesus did not allow the man to draw him into a dialogue, a crazy discourse between sanity and insanity, purity and impurity, holiness and abject horror. He just said, with incontestable authority, "Be quiet! Come out of the man" (Mark 1:25 NLT). That's it, just shut up and depart. The people were amazed to see that the demon did just that, kicking and screaming all the way. And Jesus proceeded with his ministry in the synagogue unhampered.

Those who witnessed the confrontation paid far more attention to this teacher than they normally accorded whoever stood up to comment on the Scriptures. Makes sense, doesn't it? The people witnessed a wild, unleashed demon rebuked, silenced, and reduced to helplessness. Who had such authority? Who *was* this man?

To read the story of Jesus and the evil spirit, see Mark 1:23–27 and Luke 4:33–37.

Holy Healings

Jesus Heals Peter's Mother-in-Law and Many Others on the Sabbath

REMEMBER SUNDAY DINNER at home after the church worship service each week? Perhaps it's only a sentimental memory for many today, but once upon a time it was a big deal going home from church, all gussied up, to what would certainly be the most complete, balanced, and fancy meal on the table all week. And if you brought the preacher home with you, it was all the more special.

We get the impression that it was the same in Jesus' day. The crowd of disciples, all proud of their connection with the newly recognized local teacher, followed Peter home for a Sabbath-day meal at his house. They must have been a joyful lot. Jesus had just hit two home runs in the morning synagogue service, and they were the inner circle whom he'd chosen as his teammates! But no sooner did they enter the house than someone whispered, "Peter's mother-in-law is sick." Word soon spread, and when it made its way to Jesus, it was accompanied by the implication that maybe he could "take a look" at her to see if there might be anything he could do.

When Jesus saw the woman afflicted by a high fever, he took her by the hand, murmured a brief word of rebuke to whatever was causing the fever, and lifted her up. Instantly, she was well. Accomplished hostess that she was, she immediately began to serve her guests! The rhythm of the household returned, and it was a glorious Sabbath afternoon.

As the shadows lengthened and the day drew to a close, a strange phenomenon occurred. One by one, every sick person in town quietly assembled in the front yard, waiting for the Sabbath to be officially over at sunset. Word had gotten out on the street of Jesus' healing Peter's mother-in-law. Since he had cast out a demon at the synagogue in the morning, that miracle was known too. So everyone afflicted with a fever, a withered limb, pounding headaches, demonic oppression, epilepsy—you name it—came and waited for Jesus.

The yard was soon full of noise and motion, a veritable circus of writhing, whimpering, shrieking, drooling, sick, and demon-possessed people. Jesus went around touching each one, speaking quietly, firmly, commanding the demons to leave without a word of protest. As his authority settled over the group assembled there— what amounted to almost the entire city of Capernaum—it became quiet and peaceful. By bedtime, all were well, all were grateful, all were satisfied.

To read more about this amazing day in Jesus' life, see Matthew 8:14–17; Mark 1:29–34; and Luke 4:38–41.

Fishy Stories

The Disciples Land the Biggest Catch of Their Lives

MANY FISHERMEN know the frustration of sitting in one spot for hours, hoping to land "the big one" (or sometimes *any* fish at all), and coming away with nothing. Jesus' disciples were experienced fishermen well acquainted with this frustration. But Jesus, a carpenter by trade and a Messiah by nature, had the goal of turning them into the greatest fishermen the world would ever know. Catching fish was only the beginning.

It all began on a day when Jesus taught by the Lake of Gennesaret (the Sea of Galilee). With the steadily jostling crowd jockeying to get closer to Jesus, the only place left for him to go was out on the water. There were two boats to choose from—both belonging to fishermen who were currently occupied with cleaning their nets. He chose one owned by a man named Simon.

After preaching to the crowd from the boat, Jesus made an unusual request: go further into the water and let down the nets.

Was this a sermon or a fishing lesson? Simon wasn't sure. Besides, hadn't he fished all night already without one fish to show for his troubles? But Simon obeyed, and he soon discovered one important thing: when Jesus declared that the time to fish had come, believe him. The nets were soon so full of fish that they were stretched to the point of tearing.

Simon cried out for help from the members of the other boat—James and John, the sons of Zebedee. But seeing the huge amount of fish was terrifying rather than exhilarating to Simon. It caused him to realize that he was a sinful man in the presence of a holy one.

This huge catch of fish was enough to inspire any fisherman. But Simon, James, and John were inspired to give up trawling just for fish. As Jesus said, "From now on you will catch men" (Luke 5:10 NIV). Jesus had reeled in "the big one"—a fresh catch of disciples.

The promise to catch people must have seemed farfetched years later, after Jesus was crucified. Although the disciples had seen the risen Jesus and knew that he would not be with them each day, they were no longer sure what to do with their lives. So the disciples—Peter, James, John, Thomas, Nathanael, and others—turned to the only profession they knew—fishing.

The night passed and not a fish could be coaxed into their nets. There was nothing to do but return to shore.

On the shore stood a man whose identity they couldn't make out in the early morning light.

"Haven't you any fish?" the man asked (John 21:5 NIV).

After they replied in the negative, the man said, "Throw your net on the right side of the boat and you will find some" (John 21:6).

Well, this seemed like a pretty dumb idea. After all, if there weren't any fish on the left, there weren't gonna be any fish on the right. But they decided to toss in the nets anyway. And it's a good thing too. They soon discovered an amazing catch of fish, one caught without damaging the net!

That was when they realized who the man was—Jesus!

In his excitement, Peter leaped into the water and waded to shore but soon had to climb back onto the boat to help with the fish. Someone must have quickly counted them, for the tally of fish numbered 153. Amazing!

But this adventure wasn't just about fish. It was about a Savior who could lead a sad group of men to go beyond their comfort zones and land the biggest catch of their lives. From then on, after

Jesus' return to heaven, they would catch people. And one day on Pentecost, they would land the biggest catch of all—thousands. But that's another story.

These fishing stories can be found in Luke 5:1–11 and John 21:1–14.

Willing and Able

Jesus Heals a Man with Leprosy

THE STORY OF A LEPER who came and knelt before Jesus asking to be healed of his dreaded skin disease is told three times in the Gospels of Matthew, Mark, and Luke. Though details vary slightly from writer to writer, what is identical in all three accounts is what was said. The man said clearly and unequivocally, "Lord, if you are willing, you can make me clean." And Jesus answered, "I am willing. . . . Be clean!"

So simple, so fresh, such tightly packed character development and drama! In only a smattering of words, each gospel writer shows us so much of the faith walk. In those days, lepers were outcasts, nobodies. They couldn't mix with people or make a living. They were pretty hopeless. But this one needy leper had somehow come to understand the power of God that flowed through Jesus. He knew that Jesus' power was limited only by whether he wanted to use it or not. He understood the sovereignty of God—there was no point in wheedling and begging, trying to manipulate Jesus. He had the power to heal him. It was simply a question of whether he wanted to use it for this purpose. In simple faith, the leper stated the obvious; then he humbly waited to see what would happen next.

Jesus' answer was equally brief and equally eloquent. "I am indeed willing. Yes, this is something I *want* to do. I want to see you clean . . . so *be* clean!"

How many of us doubt either one or the other elements of the leper's statement? On the one hand, we hope that Jesus would like to see us live better, more fruitful, and healthier lives, but we're not sure that he's really that involved in this world, that he really carries that much clout down here. Or, on the other hand, we agree theologically that he is Lord of the universe, but secretly doubt that he *wants* us to be whole and healthy. It would surprise some of us to hear him say of some besetting weakness or another that has plagued us for years, "I *am* willing to get rid of that for you. Let me take it. I *want* you to be clean." Instead, we plod along half convinced that Jesus could heal us if he wanted to, but only half convinced.

In the leper's case, Jesus strongly urged him to make his healing public. He told him, "Go show yourself to the priests, and make sure this whole thing is clear and above board and free of nagging questions about its validity." Just one touch by Jesus, and he was forever changed.

For more about this humble leper's miracle, read Matthew 8:1–4; Mark 1:40–45; and Luke 5:12–16.

The Man
Who Amazed Jesus

A Centurion's Faith Astounds Jesus

How could Jesus be amazed by anything? After all, he's God. Being all-knowing, nothing should surprise him. But one day, something did.

In Jesus' day, the conquering Romans ruled Palestine. While areas of Palestine were ruled by partially Jewish leaders such as King Herod, even these rulers were still under the authority of Rome. The people of Israel were used to seeing garrisons of Roman troops throughout the land.

One day while Jesus was in Capernaum, a group of Jewish leaders appeared before him on behalf of a Roman centurion (see Luke 7:1–3). That they would meet with Jesus at the request of a Gentile was amazing enough. After all, many of the Jews hated the oppressive Romans due to the cruelty they experienced. Romans could force a Jew to be a burden bearer anytime they liked and had the freedom to take whatever they wanted. Such was life in a Roman-occupied territory. But this centurion was different.

Having learned of Jesus' reputation as a miracle worker, the centurion sent the leaders to represent him before the great rabbi. These leaders had one request: could Jesus come and heal the centurion's servant? His treasured servant was near death due to a paralyzing ailment.

The Jewish leaders went on to explain how the centurion greatly helped the people of Israel by donating money to have a synagogue built. Because of his kindness, the centurion seemed a deserving candidate for a miracle.

Although Jesus agreed to go, ironically, the centurion realized his unworthiness to receive anything from Jesus. This military leader of one hundred men could have demanded that Jesus come to his house, *right now*. Instead, he said, "Lord, do not trouble yourself, for I am not worthy to have you come under my roof. Therefore I did not presume to come to you. But say the word, and let my servant be healed" (Luke 7:6–7 ESV). The centurion reasoned that Jesus had the power and authority to simply command the illness to leave and heal his servant.

Jesus was totally amazed by the centurion's response. He told his listeners, "I tell you, not even in Israel have I found such faith" (Luke 7:9). And Jesus had a message for the centurion: "Let it be done for you as you have believed" (Matthew 8:13 ESV).

The centurion's servant was healed the moment Jesus said the word—all because a Gentile had the kind of faith that amazed the Son of God.

To read more about the man who amazed Jesus, read Matthew 8:5–13 and Luke 7:1–10.

Through the Roof

N O ONE COULD GET IN. The crowds thronging around Jesus in the house were, literally, prohibitive. The four men had carried their paralyzed friend a long way. Yet when they arrived at the house where Jesus was teaching, there wasn't room for a person to turn around, let alone to carry in a pallet with a man stretched out on it.

People were packed in as tight as the little house could possibly accommodate them. A major portion of the crowd, with front-row seats, were big-shot religious teachers who had come from as far away as Jerusalem just to listen to Jesus' teaching. But the four friends weren't about to just drop their project.

What happens when an irresistible force meets an unmovable object? It goes around. The four men simply changed their procedure. This was an early example of that expression "Thinking outside the box." *If we can't get through horizontally, then what about vertically?*

They climbed up on the flat roof of the house and assessed the situation. *Hmmm. If Jesus is standing about there . . . we can go in about here.* One man began picking up the sticks and dirt piled on top of the roof tiles. Then they all started removing the roofing materials until a hole appeared, right above where Jesus was sitting.

It must have been a bit distracting—and funny—to be sitting in that room as dirt and chalk and clay began to drop from the ceiling in bits and pieces. Maybe Jesus himself had a wry grin on his face as he stopped to watch the four men, now sweating from their effort.

Slowly a long mat tipped and swayed down through the hole in the roof. The disabled man looked around sheepishly at the room full of people staring at him. Jesus' eyes were directed upward, taking in the looks of determination and hope and faith on the faces of the four friends perched precariously around the hole. They looked back at Jesus, completely sure that he was going to heal their friend. Jesus smiled. This was the kind of faith he loved to see but rarely encountered in his days on earth.

"Son," he said to the paralytic, "your sins are forgiven" (Mark 2:5 NIV).

Wait. That's odd. *Sin?* What's sin got to do with it?

Well . . . *everything.*

If you think about it, this was the most natural thing for Jesus to say. He understood what most of us don't—that our greatest problem is our sin. We struggle all our lives with the ramifications and consequences of sin. And we get so caught up in trying to untangle ourselves from all *that,* that we seldom concentrate on the heart of the problem, the source of all our woes, sin itself.

But the religious elite sitting there were aghast. "Why does this fellow talk like that? He's blaspheming! Who can forgive sins but God alone?" They were highly offended.

In the meantime, the paralyzed man was still lying there on the pallet. The men on the roof above were beginning to lose their smiles.

So Jesus explained. "Look," he said, "which is easier: to grant forgiveness of sins or to tell a paralyzed man to rise up and walk? I want you to understand that you're right, only God can forgive sins . . . and that's why *I* can forgive sins. So to prove that this man's sins are forgiven (something you can't see), I'll prove my authority by making him walk (something you *can* see)."

And so it was. The man stood right up, picked up his mat, and carried it out through the crowd. Everyone, Scripture says, *every-*

one glorified God that day! You can't argue with that kind of evidence!

To read more about Jesus, the paralyzed man, and his fabulous four friends, see Matthew 9:1–8; Mark 2:1–12; and Luke 5:17–26.

Girl, Get Up!

A Synagogue Official's Dead Daughter Returns to Life

"NO PARENT should have to bury their child." Thus spoke Theoden, King of Rohan, at the funeral of his son, Théodred. If you saw *The Lord of the Rings: The Two Towers*, the movie based on J.R.R. Tolkien's novel, you witnessed the sad spectacle of a broken father after the interment of his only child.

Death is one of the harsh realities of planet Earth. And Jairus, a synagogue ruler in Jesus' day, was about to get a taste of this harsh reality. His daughter was dying.

Like most parents, he would have moved heaven and earth if he could have to get help for his child. And thankfully, there was a slice of heaven right there on earth: Jesus. *Jesus could do something,* he reasoned.

We don't have to have a child of our own to get a sense of this man's desperation. The Gospel of Mark has the play-by-play: "Seeing Jesus, he fell at his feet and pleaded earnestly with him, 'My little daughter is dying'" (Mark 5:22–23 NIV).

Now Jesus was always one to show compassion. Off he went with Jairus to make a house call. If this were a movie, the hopeful notes of a flute or a violin would sound as Jairus probably breathed fully for the first time since his daughter became ill. But the hopeful strains were about to turn somber as the synagogue leader was informed of the worst before he could make it home: his daughter was dead.

Too late. No need for you, Jesus. It's over. That's what the mourners who gave Jairus the news believed.

Imagine this father walking in the door to face the cold, still form of his child. Whether or not this was his only child, the Bible does not say. What it does say is that he didn't have to walk in alone. Jesus kept walking into the house, past the wailing mourners.

After Jesus pointedly told them that the little girl was asleep, rather than dead, you can imagine how his remark impacted the crowd. Their mourning turned to laughter at his expense. After throwing everyone out of the house except for the parents and his disciples, Jesus went into the child's room.

There it was—every parent's nightmare had come to pass. The child lay on the bed, no breath of life stirring. Never again would they smooth her hair, wipe her tears, or listen to her chatter. But Jesus then did a very strange thing. He took the child's hand, and with power in his voice said, "Little girl, I say to you, get up!" (Mark 5:41).

The girl stood. She was twelve years old and would see her thirteenth birthday someday.

Jesus could have echoed Theoden's words, "No parent should have to bury their child." That day, a parent didn't have to.

This girl gets a second chance at life in Matthew 9:18–19, 23–26; Mark 5:21–24, 35–43; and Luke 8:40–42, 49–56.

A Break from Bleeding

The Touch That Brings Healing

ISN'T IT INTERESTING how an ordinary day can turn extraordinary with the right encounter with the right person? There are some people whose ordinary days are extraordinarily painful. Jesus had an encounter with a woman like that.

It all started with a crowd of people pushing, straining closer, just to catch a glimpse of Jesus. To say that he was popular was an understatement. He'd performed miracles that everyone talked about. Crowds followed him—he was the rock star of his day; the celebrity doctor who made house calls.

In fact, he was on his way to a house call, responding to a synagogue leader who begged him to *please* come and heal his sick daughter (see "Girl, Get Up!" p. 221). But he couldn't get away from the crowds. People touched him, possibly whispering to him, "Help me," "Help my friend." So many needs, so much pain.

But suddenly, he felt a different kind of touch, one that *drew* power from him. He turned, asking his disciples a question that seemed stunningly obvious: "Who touched my clothes?" (Mark 5:30 CEV). Duh! *Everyone*, Jesus!

The story pivots as Jesus did, searching the crowd to find out who touched him. He had only to look as far as the nearest patch of ground, where he finds the woman whose extraordinarily painful day had intersected with his.

Who was she? An unnamed woman who had a problem—a major, life-draining problem. She'd been bleeding for twelve years and had given everything she had to find the cure that continually eluded her. She was so tired, so humiliated, so lonely.

And then Jesus came to town.

If only . . . if only I could touch even the fringe of his clothes, she reasoned. But touching anyone, especially such a holy man, well, it just wasn't prudent. After all, she was unclean. Bleeding rendered her unclean, according to Jewish laws. She *shouldn't* touch *anyone.* But if only . . . if only she could just touch him, she would be healed.

She reached out and touched.

Now Jesus was asking, "Who touched me?"

Busted. Was she in trouble now? She had to confess. "I did it. I touched you." The words choked out of her; the fear of discovery made her tremble. She looked at his feet rather than into his eyes.

But Jesus didn't yell, didn't accuse. Instead, he said, "Daughter, your faith has healed you. Go in peace and be freed from your suffering" (Mark 5:34 NIV). He said those words in front of everyone to show that the faith of one person could evoke the power of God.

Now she could look into his eyes—such eyes of compassion. Her ordinary and painful day was now indelibly beautiful.

The account of this extraordinary day can be found in Matthew 9:20–22; Mark 5:24–34; and Luke 8:43–48.

A Handful of Hope

Jesus Heals a Man's Deformed Hand on the Sabbath

IT WAS OBVIOUSLY A SETUP. The scribes and Pharisees were already there, waiting and watching. So was a man with a conspicuously deformed hand, sitting near the front where he could not be overlooked. The only person missing was the Teacher. The religious leaders noted his arrival with cruel and malicious impatience.

The religious leaders wanted this confrontation. They hoped that Jesus would perform this healing. Then they'd have grounds for an arrest. After all, it was against the law to do any work on the Sabbath. And healing, well, that was work, right? Even though Jesus never broke a sweat when he healed someone—he was *doing* something, so that was good enough for an arrest. And that was all that mattered to these guys.

While author Luke comments that "Jesus knew their thoughts" (Luke 6:8 NLT), the account in the book of Matthew reports that they actually took the initiative on the matter, and provoked him. With the poor man sitting there as prominent as a pimple, the "Pharisees asked Jesus, 'Does the law permit a person to work by healing on the Sabbath?' [They were hoping he would say yes, so they could bring charges against him]" (Matthew 12:10 NLT).

Jesus came right back at them with irrefutable logic based on their own experience: "If you had a sheep that fell into a well on the Sabbath, wouldn't you work to pull it out? Of course you would. And how much more valuable is a person than a sheep!

Yes, the law permits a person to do good on the Sabbath" (Matthew 12:11–12).

The Pharisees had no answer for him. They maintained a bitter and stony silence that resonated in the synagogue for several moments. Jesus waited, angry and grieving their hard, hard hearts (see Mark 3:5). Finally the impasse was broken as Jesus said to the man, "Hold out your hand." He did, and of course, his hand was restored to fullness and health just like his other hand!

But this story concludes in a minor key with the bitterness of Jesus' enemies unabated. Rather than report, as the gospel writers often do, the happy response of the crowd at Jesus' wonder-working, all three Gospels report with a certain gloominess that the Pharisees went out and took counsel to try to figure out how they could *destroy* Jesus. They had set a trap; Jesus had walked right into it, healed a man, and walked right back out again. They couldn't stand it. "He's got to go!" they concluded unanimously.

But one man there that day went away with a big handful of hope.

To read more about this miraculous healing and Jesus' confrontation with the Pharisees, see Matthew 12:9–14; Mark 3:1–6; and Luke 6:6–11.

Reach Out
and Touch Someone

Jesus Heals All Who Touch Him

ONE OF THE THINGS about Jesus' healing ministry that stands out from the pages of Scripture is that he seemed to be so indiscriminate about it all. To twenty-first century would-be patients accustomed to filling out endless medical papers and fulfilling requirements of PPOs and HMOs, it is astonishing to see Jesus reach out and heal, and heal, and heal, . . . without asking questions of the afflicted or giving them prerequisite conditions.

Anybody and everybody who had any kind of medical condition was eligible for healing from Jesus. This particular day, no sooner did Jesus get out of the boat than they recognized him. "They ran throughout that whole region and carried the sick on mats to wherever they heard he was. And wherever he went—into villages, towns or countryside—they placed the sick in the marketplaces. They begged him to let them touch even the edge of his cloak, and all who touched him were healed" (Mark 6:55–56 NIV).

There in the middle of the great eddy of whirling bodies the figure of Jesus bent over first this one and then that one, administering healing and restoration to disfigured bodies and proffering peace and calm to troubled spirits. As he moved through the crowd, touching one after another of the hundreds of needy, trembling bodies, a great calm and quiet rippled from the center where he was, out toward the edges where some still waited to be healed. As he passed by, those on the sides of the path reached out and touched his garment in faith as he walked by, and they, too, were healed!

By the time he finished the day, *everyone* had received what he or she needed. "All who touched him were healed." It was an amazing 100 percent performance, the likes of which no one had ever seen.

To read more about this amazing day of miracles, see Matthew 14:34–36 and Mark 6:53–56.

The Faith of Bartimaeus

A Blind Man Sees

PICTURE A WORLD painfully, unrelentingly dark—a darkness stretching beyond clouds hiding the sun or the blackest of midnights. Every day you stretch out your hand, hoping that someone will take it and lead you where you need to go or throw you enough money to buy some food.

Welcome to the world of blind Bartimaeus in the first century.

In the city of Jericho, blind Bartimaeus, the son of Timaeus,

could usually be found on the road just outside the city. His occupation was begging—the only occupation available for a blind man.
With crowds going in and out of the city of Jericho, perhaps someone would have pity.

As you see Bartimaeus waiting by the side of the road, let your
imagination pan to the city in the background. Leaving the city is a
crowd of people. Nothing new here. But in the forefront of the
crowd is a man—a man who is the reason for the crowd. He is
Jesus, the famous rabbi and healer. With him are his disciples, who
are usually good at keeping the paparazzi at bay.

Here he comes, closer and closer.

When someone whispers to Bartimaeus that the Teacher is
here, hope loosens Bartimaeus's tongue. "Son of David, Jesus, have
mercy on me!" (Mark 10:47 HCSB).

But the crowd is not letting him get away with disturbing the
peace. "Hush! Don't bother him!" To them, he is an embarrassment. Can't he understand that he's making a fool of himself in
front of such a well-respected Teacher who has visited their fair
city?

Their words cause him to shout louder and louder. After all,
Jesus was the one who quoted the words of the prophet Isaiah, "The
Spirit of the Lord is on Me, because He has anointed Me to preach
good news to the poor. He has sent Me to proclaim freedom to the
captives and recovery of sight to the blind, to set free the oppressed" (Luke 4:18 HCSB). *Recovery of sight to the blind.*

But wait. Jesus stops and asks for Bartimaeus to be brought to
him. Not wasting any time, Bartimaeus hurries to Jesus, wishing
that he could see his face. Perhaps he could . . . if only Jesus would
give him the gift of sight. When he is asked what he wants from
Jesus, Bartimaeus has only one request: *to see.*

"Go your way," Jesus says. "Your faith has healed you" (Mark
10:52 HCSB).

And with that, he is healed, from the word *Go!*

Imagine you are Bartimaeus as the darkness recedes and retinas, which previously recorded no images, now begin to function. They interpret the image before you as that of a man, the first man you've ever seen in your life. The face of the one you would follow—you *will* follow—anywhere.

The darkness recedes for Bartimaeus in Matthew 20:29–34; Mark 10:46–52; and Luke 18:35–43.

Say What?

Jesus Heals the Deaf Man Who Has a Speech Impediment

THIS HEALING STORY is considerably different from many others in the Gospels. It takes place in Gentile territory, yet it is plainly Aramaic that Jesus speaks to the person with whom he is dealing (Mark translates it). Rather than approach Jesus on his own, the man was brought to Jesus by an unnamed crowd of people to whom Jesus gives his attention before and after the miracle, addressing "them," not the man made whole, with the word of warning not to publish the miracle abroad.

When Jesus returned from the Gentile territory of Tyre and Sidon, he made his way around the lake to another Gentile territory, the ten Greek cities east of the Sea of Galilee known as the Decapolis. There a crowd met him, bringing him a deaf man whose tongue was somewhat paralyzed. Not only was he deaf, but he could not speak clearly either, a common and understandable combination.

They asked Jesus to lay hands on him—an interesting request. We wonder what they sought, exactly, for they were eventually astonished by the results, which evidently exceeded their expectations. Jesus complied with their request, taking the man into his own hands and leading him away from the crowd.

When they'd established what Jesus apparently considered a discrete distance between them and the onlookers, Jesus began to earnestly relate to the deaf man. He put one hand on either side of his head and thrust his fingers into the man's ears. Then he let fall a gob of his own saliva onto the man's tongue. Strange way to administer a healing from one who sometimes merely spoke a word and people miles away were healed by his authority!

While we can only speculate on why Jesus behaved this particular way on this particular occasion, what seems clear is that Jesus became deeply, personally involved in the man's predicament. This was no mere perfunctory dismissal of some ailment or affliction, performed almost unconsciously while Jesus directed his primary attention to some other agenda. The Gospel of Mark shows us Jesus getting "down and dirty," focusing all his energies on the man in front of him. He was right up close, face-to-face, doing literal "hands-on" adjustments to the man's dysfunction. The intensity culminated when Jesus, after he'd done everything he could outwardly, looked up to heaven and let out a deep sigh. It was an audible manifestation of the intense personal engagement Jesus had with the act of releasing the man from his suffering.

"*Ephphatha,*" Jesus said, "which means, 'Be opened!'" (Mark 7:34 NLT). Immediately both the man's ears and his tongue were released, and he began to speak plainly. Not a trace of the former impediment could be heard, and those who'd brought him to Jesus were flabbergasted by the sound of the man's clear elocution. Perhaps they recalled the clear allusion to such a miracle in Isaiah's prophecy of the Messiah to come: "And when he comes, he will open the eyes of the blind and unplug the ears of the deaf" (Isaiah 35:5 NLT).

And though Jesus sternly warned them not to tell it around, the more he admonished them to keep quiet, the more they told the story!

To find out more about the deaf man's story, read Mark 7:31–37.

The Ol' Spit and Polish

Jesus Heals a Blind Man in an Unusual Way

I F SOMEONE SPIT in our face, most of us would have a less than gracious response. But for a blind man in the town of Bethsaida, one memory he held dear was the day someone spit in his face.

While Jesus traveled with his disciples, it was not uncommon for people to bring others to him in the hope that he would heal them. As Jesus entered Bethsaida, his attention was arrested by some people who brought a blind man before him.

Now Bethsaida was one of the cities where many of Jesus' miracles had been performed, yet the people had remained unchanged in their thinking. This grieved Jesus' heart (see Matthew 11:21). That day in Bethsaida, however, he was there to help and heal in response to a group of folks who believed he could do something.

Instead of getting right to it, Jesus took the man's hand and led him *out* of the city. Was he hoping to avoid publicity? Was the climate of unbelief grievous to him? Either way, to the outskirts Jesus went with the blind man. Rather than telling the man, "Receive your sight" or "Your faith has healed you," as he said on other occasions, Jesus did another strange thing: he spit on the man's eyes!

In ancient Jewish culture, spitting into a person's face was usually a way to publicly shame that person (see Numbers 12:14; Deuteronomy 25:9). Jesus was well aware of the cultural implications. However, he was never one to shy away from controversy. His task was to heal, not humiliate.

After placing his hands on the man's eyes, he asked, "Do you [possibly] see anything?" (Mark 8:23 AMP). Jesus had healed other blind people (see "The Faith of Bartimaeus," p. 228), but he hadn't asked that question before.

The man peered intently and responded that he did, sort of. "I see people, but [they look] like trees walking" (Mark 8:24).

Hmm. Tricky. His response merited a second touch from Jesus. This time, he could see clearly! Jesus then warned the man against going back to town and blabbing the news (which might possibly put Jesus' life in danger before he was ready). A rather subdued ending for an unusual adventure.

Read about this two-part healing in Mark 8:22–26.

Talkin' in the Coffin

When a Widow's Son Dies, Jesus Brings Him Back to Life

WITHOUT FAMILIES, widows during Bible times could not support themselves. This is why a childless widow usually was among the poorest of the poor in Palestine. Widows could glean the leftover grain in fields (see Deuteronomy 24:19–21; Ruth 2:2–3), but other than that, they had no source of income. But God had compassion on his people. The law of Moses included commands to help the poor, the widows, and foreigners in the land. Sadly, though, some widows fell through the cracks of the system.

So imagine the plight of the woman walking behind a coffin as the crowd followed her out of the town of Nain. Not only was she a widow, but her son—her only son—was now dead. All hope for her own survival was dead too.

There are some moments in life when two paths intersect and lives are changed. This was one of those moments. The widow's path happened to cross that of Jesus, who approached the town just as she was leaving the city gate. Nothing strikes the heart of God more than the pain of his people. As David, one of Israel's greatest kings, described in one of his psalms, "The LORD is close to the brokenhearted; he rescues those whose spirits are crushed" (Psalm 34:18 NLT).

Jesus understood the widow's agony. "Don't cry" (Luke 7:13 NIV), he said. This was not an empty "There, there" kind of condolence, but a foreshadowing of something coming. Despair was simply not on Jesus' agenda for that day—not for this woman.

Touching the coffin, Jesus said, "Young man, I say to you, get up!" (Luke 7:14).

The widow's son returned to life, just like that. And he not only sat up, he also began to talk to everyone! Imagine the widow's change of countenance. Imagine the remarks of the people with her as they returned to Nain. What began as a funeral march became a march of joy. That day in Nain there was one less grave to mark.

For more about this amazing story of death and life, read Luke 7:11–17.

JESUS' DISCIPLES

Following is the list of Jesus' twelve disciples and some key verses about them. Lists of the disciples are also found in Matthew 10:1–4; Mark 3:16–19; Luke 6:14–16; and Acts 1:13.

DISCIPLE	SOME KEY FACTS	REFERENCES
Simon (Peter)	Leader of the early church; called Jesus the Messiah	Matthew 4:18–20 Mark 8:29–33 Luke 22:31–34 John 21:15–19 Acts 2:14–41; 10:1–11:8
Andrew (Peter's brother)	Brought Peter to Jesus	Matthew 4:18–20 John 1:35–42; 6:8–9; 12:20–24
James (son of Zebedee)	One of the three core disciples; beheaded by Herod	Matthew 4:21–22 Mark 10:35–40 Luke 9:52–56 Acts 12:1–2

Disciple	Some Key Facts	References
John (son of Zebedee)	One of the three core disciples; wrote the Gospel of John	Matthew 4:21–22 Mark 1:19; 10:35–40 Luke 9:52–56 John 19:26–27; 21:20–24
Matthew (Levi)	Former tax collector; wrote the Gospel of Matthew	Matthew 9:9–13 Mark 2:15–17 Luke 5:27–32
Philip	Brought Nathanael to Jesus	John 1:43–46; 6:2–7; 12:20–22; 14:8–11
Bartholomew (Nathanael)	Initially skeptical of Jesus' claims	John 1:45–51; 21:1–13
Thomas (the Twin)	Doubted that Jesus rose	John 14:5; 20:24–29; 21:1–13
James (son of Alphaeus)	Unknown	None beyond the lists noted above
Thaddaeus (Judas son of James)	Unknown	John 14:22
Simon (the Zealot)	Committed to the cause of his people's freedom	None beyond the lists noted above
Judas Iscariot	Betrayed Jesus; killed himself	Matthew 26:20–25 Luke 22:47–48 John 12:4–8

Finally, Freedom

On the Sabbath, Jesus Heals a Woman Crippled by an Evil Spirit

EIGHTEEN YEARS is a long time to be bent over, never able to stand up straight. After a while maybe one gets used to it, seeing the whole world from that weirdly distorted perspective, looking up sideways at everyone from that painful folded posture. But you know, this woman would have given anything to stand up straight like everyone else, look people in the eye, lay her head back and laugh upright at the sky like when she was a little girl.

Jesus was in the middle of teaching in the synagogue on the Sabbath when he noticed her. Most people would have made a mental note of her condition and perhaps resolved to say a prayer for her later. But no one would have stopped the whole synagogue proceedings to call attention to her affliction.

But Jesus did. He called out to her and then approached her. In the gender-separated synagogue, this would have meant either his passing into the women's court (a balcony with wooden curtains from behind which the women could follow the proceedings down on the floor where the males were gathered), or else calling her to come into the synagogue proper so that he could put his hands on her and, literally, straighten her out. When he did so, he said with authority, "Woman, you are set free from your infirmity" (Luke 13:12 NIV). She found herself standing perfectly straight and tall for the first time in eighteen years. Naturally, she began to praise God in a loud voice.

Between her enthusiastic praises and the shocked buzz of those in attendance, the room suddenly became very noisy and very disorderly. The guy in charge rushed to the center of the room and called for a little decorum. Though he did not dare address either Jesus or the woman directly, he stated to the onlookers in a general way, "Look, any of you who want to be healed, there are six working days in the week. Come here *then* to be healed if you want to be healed, but not on the Sabbath." It was as close to a direct rebuke as he could bring himself to utter.

But Jesus was having none of it, and said in so many words: "You've got to be kidding, you hypocrite!" he said. "Doesn't each and every one of you untie his donkey or his ox on the Sabbath and let them go get a drink? So why shouldn't this daughter of Abraham, whom Satan has had bound up for eighteen long years be untied from her bonds and set free on a Sabbath? What a ridiculous and petty view you have of God's laws! If you have mercy on your thirsty donkey, won't God have mercy on this suffering woman?"

As usually happened, Jesus' adversaries burned with shame and inwardly resolved all the more to get vengeance on this rabble-rouser who made them feel that way.

The rest of the observers, the common people, rejoiced in seeing Jesus heal suffering people.

To read more about the crippled woman, see Luke 13:10–17.

Dealing with Dropsy

When Jesus Heals, the Pharisees Squeal

B EING AT a formal dinner party is hard enough without the added stress of being watched. Whenever he was invited over for a meal, Jesus was usually watched quite carefully. Oh, not because he failed to use the right utensil (dinner parties back then didn't have that added stress), and not because he monopolized the conversation. The Pharisees and other Jewish leaders watched Jesus, hoping to find something—anything—they could use as ammunition against the popular teacher/healer who had the nerve to declare himself to be the promised Messiah. Worst of all, he sometimes healed people on the Sabbath! This was a definite no-no in their book. After all, healing constituted work. And on the Sabbath, no one was supposed to work.

So, while partaking of the Sabbath meal at the home of a fellow Pharisee, the other Jewish leaders eyed Jesus closely. Would Jesus slip up and heal someone? Would he finally say something they could refute?

Jesus was on the watch as well, having noticed a man who had a condition known as dropsy. We would call this an edema or a build-up of fluids caused by congestive heart failure or some other issue. How fitting that Luke, the gospel writer and a physician, would note this case, which would have made the medical journals had they been published at that time.

Why was the man there? Was this a setup to provide Jesus with just enough rope to hang himself through kindness? The text does not say. As usual, Jesus was not one to simply notice a problem. He did something about it, regardless of the danger to himself. First, he asked the Jewish leaders, "Is it lawful to heal on the Sabbath, or not?" (Luke 14:3 ESV). Talk about courting controversy! But his remark inspired silence, rather than speeches.

Perhaps a pin dropping could be heard in the room as Jesus touched the man, imparting his healing strength. The silence continued with Jesus' next statement: "Which of you, having a son or an ox that has fallen into a well on a Sabbath day, will not immediately pull him out?" (Luke 14:5). In other words, wouldn't you take the route of mercy rather than legalism? In the Pharisees' case, the answer was option B—legalism.

The man formerly suffering from dropsy went away healed. But the Pharisees just went away more determined to do something about Jesus.

To read about when Jesus healed the man with dropsy, see Luke 14:1–6.

An Attitude of Gratitude

Ten Lepers Are Healed, but Only One Says, "Thanks"

BACK IN BIBLE TIMES, well before the advent of incurable diseases such as AIDS, the most virulent disease was leprosy

(Hansen's disease). Due to the highly communicable nature of the disease and the lack of antibiotics, lepers were forced to live outside of society in accordance with the law of Moses (see Leviticus 13–14). Individuals with any type of infectious skin ailment were considered unclean and could not be touched by others as long as they had the disease. Once they were cured, they were to go to the priest and be pronounced clean. But unless that happened (what were the chances?), they had to walk around calling out, "Unclean! Unclean!" as a warning to others.

Once Jesus was passing through a village between Samaria and Galilee and found himself face-to-face with ten lepers. But instead of calling out, "Unclean, unclean," these lepers yelled out their request: "Jesus, Master, have pity on us!" (Luke 17:13 NIV). Undoubtedly they knew about Jesus' reputation as a healer. If anyone could cure them, he could.

The compassionate Savior didn't keep them in suspense. He told them, "Go, show yourselves to the priests" (Luke 17:14)—a command in keeping with the law of Moses. As the lepers obediently headed off to find the nearest priest, the miracle happened. They found themselves more cured of their disease with each step. Their lives were now free of the terrible stigma of leprosy. End of story.

Except that it wasn't. One of the former lepers ran back to find Jesus. Casting himself on the ground before Jesus—a position of absolute humility—he offered profuse thanks and praise to God.

Jesus commented, "Were not all ten cleansed? Where are the other nine? Was no one found to return and give praise to God except this foreigner?" (Luke 17:17–18). This "foreigner" was a Samaritan. Although the Samaritans and the Jews were related, the Samaritans were considered "half Jews" due to the intermarriage of Israelites and Assyrians centuries before. So Jews and Samaritans didn't usually socialize with one another. The Jews went out of their way to avoid entering Samaria—the territory of the Samaritans. But here was one who showed an attitude of deep gratitude.

In response to the man's gratitude, Jesus commended his faith, which made him physically well and possibly spiritually well also. A little bit of gratitude goes a long way.

To read more about the lepers, see Luke 17:11–19.

An Earache Erased

Jesus Heals a Soldier's Ear

MALCHUS, servant of high priest Caiaphas, must have wondered what he'd gotten himself into as he marched along with the raggedy retinue of temple guards and vigilantes out into the dark Judean countryside. Jesus was reported by one of his disciples to be in the Garden of Gethsemane, and it was toward that rendezvous point that the renegade disciple, Judas Iscariot, led them now. Malchus was nervous; his list of duties in the high priest's household did not normally include "rounding up suspected heretics and bringing them in for trial." He didn't know quite what to expect. But they had weapons, just in case.

Suddenly Jesus himself appeared in the torchlight, striding directly toward them. He seemed unperturbed by their menacing swords, clubs, and other makeshift weapons. He even seemed to have been expecting them. He coolly received Judas's kiss of greeting, which was the signal for the band of guards and household servants to grab Jesus and haul him away.

But when that first act of violence exploded, so did Jesus' friend and disciple Peter. He whipped out his sword, swung it high over Malchus's head, and brought it crashing down. He intended, no doubt, to split Malchus's head in two! But whether the dark obscured his aim or simply for lack of practice and skill, he missed his mark by about three inches, and the sword came whistling down the side of the servant's face, neatly slicing his ear off.

It was the first blood of battle, what usually triggered the instincts of warriors on both sides of a conflict into fierce attack. But Jesus' voice rang out in the dark authoritatively, "Enough of this!" His disciples automatically stopped and listened to him for their next move.

"Put your sword back in its sheath," he said to Peter, and now even his enemies were stopped cold and stunned by the sheer authority of his commanding voice.

Malchus lay on the ground, clutching the side of his head as blood spurted out. The intense pain was making him dizzy. Then Jesus walked over to him. Malchus looked up as Jesus reached down, pulled Malchus's bloody hand away from the side of his head, and then put his own hand over the wound. Malchus felt the pulsing blood stop and the pain disappear. Could that be a look of kindness on Jesus' face? Right *now*, even as he was being arrested?

Then Jesus stood back up and turned his attention to the small army of would-be bounty hunters. "What are you doing out here in the middle of the night carrying sticks and spears and coming after me like you were trying to capture a mad dog? I've been in the temple teaching every day. Why didn't you come and get me then? It would have been easier than all this melodrama," his arm swept across the scene including Malchus, who was still fingering his new ear in wonder and awe, "treating me as if I were a fugitive criminal." Malchus and the others were embarrassed, chagrined, rebuked in their spirits. But they had a job to do, and Jesus did not resist them. In fact, he acceded to their task: "But this is your hour," he said wryly, "do your worst."

So they buckled up their courage and hauled Jesus away to the high priest's house, where that official and his cronies were waiting. It was going to be a long night. But Malchus kept fingering his brand-new ear with wonder and amazement.

This story of Malchus's new ear appears in Luke 22:47–51.

One Hundred Percent Proof

Jesus Performs His First Recorded Miracle at a Wedding

THE IDIOM "the proof of the pudding is in the eating" is a fancy way of saying that the worth of an item can be measured when you see it in action. The same could be said of Jesus in his day. If people wanted 100 percent proof that Jesus was the Messiah, they had only to see him in action.

Weddings in Bible times were big social events involving days of festivities. And who better to invite to those festivities than the up-and-coming rabbi, Jesus, and his followers?

Jesus' mother was also among those invited. It was she who made known to Jesus the dilemma of the host: the wine was all gone.

In our day, this would have been the signal to end the wedding reception and send everyone home with their wedding favors. During this time, however, running out of wine caused great embarrassment for the family of the bridal party, who had a social obligation to provide enough food and drink for all. But Mary knew something the family didn't know: Jesus could do something about this. She quickly ran over to her son and told him about the problem.

Jesus did not immediately leap into action. "Dear woman, that's not our problem. . . . My time has not yet come" (John 2:4 NLT). His response to his mom may seem puzzling or disrespectful. But as someone used to continually seeking the Father's will and timing his every move, Jesus merely expressed caution. Mary waited with anticipation, knowing that he would act.

Jesus went over to the six water jars standing nearby and told the servants to fill the jars again with water. After that was done, Jesus instructed them to take some of it out and give it to the man in charge of the banquet. Once again, the servants obeyed.

When the banquet master tasted what the servants handed him, he was pleasantly surprised but not to the extent of the servants. They knew what he didn't know—that the water had been changed into *wine.* Here was 100 percent proof, in more ways than one, that Jesus was something special.

The banquet master immediately cornered the bridegroom. "A host always serves the best wine first. . . . Then, when everyone has had a lot to drink, he brings out the less expensive wine. But you have kept the best until now!" (John 2:10).

What a testimony to the goodness of a Messiah who came to enable his people to have "a rich and satisfying life" (John 10:10).

For the whole water-to-wine story, read John 2:1–11.

A Son Survives

Jesus Heals a Palace Official's Son, but Sorrows over Unbelief

"HOMETOWN HERO HONORED." This was a headline Jesus would never read in the *Galilean Gazette*. Sadly, he knew better than anyone else that hometown heroes—particularly a hometown hero calling himself the Messiah—often had to make do without the applause of the crowd.

Jesus earned the applause of many because of what he could do, not for who he claimed to be—the Savior who would someday die for the sins of all. He could perform great wonders, which inspired the welcome of the people in Galilee. Bring on the miracles, Jesus! Woo hoo! But Jesus wasn't fooled by such a welcome, knowing the unbelief that lay behind it.

During a stopover at Cana, the town in Galilee most noted as the site of Jesus' first recorded miracle (see "One Hundred Percent Proof," p. 244), an opportunity for performing another great wonder presented itself.

An official from Herod's court had a son who was deathly ill in Capernaum. Would Jesus come—please come—and heal him?

Imagine the headlines such a healing would inspire. Such good publicity this would mean for Jesus, the up-and-coming healer, especially if he pulled off healing the son of such an important man. But Jesus was not out for kudos from palace officials or any other movers and shakers. He cared only for his Father's approval.

Jesus' words, "Unless you [people] see signs and wonders, you will not believe" (John 4:48 HCSB), might have sounded harsh in the face of a father's worry over his son. But Jesus spoke the truth.

The official didn't back down, despite Jesus' rebuke. He continued to urge Jesus to come and heal his son. Always full of mercy, Jesus soon assured him that his son would survive.

As the official returned home, he was met by servants who gave him the happy news: his son was indeed alive! Learning at what hour the healing occurred, the palace official received the astounding news that his son was healed the moment Jesus told the official that his son would live.

From that point on, the palace official and his family believed in Jesus. But he proved Jesus' point. Until he saw the great wonder, he hadn't believed. Now, he did.

To read the story of the government official's son, see John 4:46–54.

No Excuses Necessary

A Man Makes Excuses Instead of Asking to Be Healed

D O YOU WANT to get well?" Jesus asked the man. At the pool of Bethesda, a question such as this probably seemed too much like stating the obvious. After all, wasn't that why disabled people came to the pool—to be healed by the waters? But Jesus, who never did anything haphazardly, had a good reason for asking.

Throughout the world there are "healing" springs where many go to soak in the waters to find relief from ailments. In Jesus' day, many with ailments were brought to the pool of Bethesda in Jerusalem. Supposedly the stirring of the water indicated the touch of an angel, and the first person into the pool when that happened would be healed. One of these sick people was a man who had been brought to the pool for thirty-eight years. But life was about to change on the day Jesus arrived.

Having learned of the man's thirty-eight years of sickness, Jesus asked the question that might have seemed rude or nonsensical, "Do you want to get well?" Jesus healed the blind, the lame, and the demon-possessed. But only with this man does the Bible text mention Jesus asking such a question.

Instead of answering, "Yes!" the man burst into a litany of excuses. "I don't have a man to put me into the pool when the water is stirred up, but while I'm coming, someone goes down ahead of me" (John 5:7 HCSB). These excuses provide a clue as to why Jesus' question was necessary.

Jesus didn't respond to the excuses or the fact that the man didn't seem to know him by reputation. Instead he said, "Get up, pick up your bedroll and walk!" (John 5:8).

At the word of Jesus, the man stood and picked up his bedroll. Despite that the man didn't ask to be healed, he was.

But lurking in the shadows were the Jewish leaders who loved to nitpick. Carrying a mat was considered "work" in their eyes. No one was supposed to work on the Sabbath.

Instead of rejoicing at the miracle from God, they demanded to know who would dare order this man to work on the Sabbath. But the healed man could not identify his healer.

Jesus eventually saw the man again and warned him against doing wrong. While the text does not go into detail as to why this warning was necessary, the fact that the man immediately identified

Jesus to the Jewish leaders leaves us wondering whether the man should have taken Jesus' advice to heart. He was physically well, but probably still sick at heart.

To read more about the lame man at the pool, read John 5:1–15.

A Sight for Sore Eyes

Jesus Uses a Mud Pie to Heal a Blind Man

IS THERE ANYTHING about yourself that you would change in a heartbeat if you could? Some might not like the noses they have or their eye color. Jesus met a man who wished he could exchange his eyes for others—eyes that could see.

One day at the temple, Jesus encountered a man who had been born blind. Jesus' disciples asked Jesus who was at fault for the man's blindness. They wondered whether or not the man's blindness was due to a sin of the parents or his own.

While that question might seem strange to us, consider how we often blame ourselves or relatives for the way we turned out. *If it hadn't been for you, I wouldn't have this emotional baggage. If Dad hadn't been such a louse, I wouldn't keep picking the wrong guy!*

Jesus quickly derailed the blame train by saying, "You're asking the wrong question. You're looking for someone to blame. There is no such cause-effect here. Look instead for what God can do" (John 9:3 MSG).

To show what God could do, Jesus spit on the ground to make mud. But making mud pies in this unconventional way was not his goal. He took the mud and placed it on the man's eyes. If you read "The Ol' Spit and Polish" (p. 232), you know that Jesus used spit once before to heal a blind man. But instead of asking this man if he saw anything, Jesus had only a command: Go wash off in the pool of Siloam.

The man didn't argue—he hit the pool. That had to be the best time anyone spent at the pool. By the time he finished, he could see!

It's hard to imagine what it must have been like for this man to see the blue sky or an emerald field of grass or a baby's smile for the first time ever. Did he laugh? Did he leap in the air? Did he cry for joy? The Bible doesn't say.

Now imagine someone you know who'd once been blind now freely walking around without a white cane and even looking you in the eye. What would you do? The man's friends couldn't believe he was the same man. Certainly those who had seen him begging at the temple day after day—as those who were blind or sick usually did—could not believe he was the same person.

Perhaps it would have been better had the story ended there— with the triumph of the gift of sight. But no. The dark clouds threatened to rain on that parade in the form of the Pharisees, who suddenly noticed two things: (1) a blind man could now see; and (2) Jesus made mud on the Sabbath day. Making mud to heal people constituted "work" in their eyes. That was a no-no on the Sabbath.

Of course they had to investigate the matter. (Getting a Spanish Inquisition vibe right about now?) The Pharisees found the formerly blind man and his parents and questioned them closely about who performed the miracle granting the man sight. Because the Pharisees' decrees were the law of the land, the man's parents were pretty scared. After all, the Pharisees could have them thrown out of the synagogue. This would mean they could no longer worship at the synagogue every week. So they put the onus squarely on their son.

The man didn't know who healed him, but he steadfastly believed that he was a prophet sent from God. In disgust, the Pharisees threw him out of the synagogue.

Jesus, of course, heard about the man's plight and went to talk to him, revealing that he was indeed the Messiah sent from God. Although the man no longer had a synagogue home, he had a Savior.

It's interesting that the story ends with yet another bitter encounter between Jesus and the Pharisees. Although he healed the blind man, he couldn't heal the Pharisees' hard hearts. They were the blind leading the blind.

Read about these blind encounters in John 9:1–41.

Lazarus Lives!

Jesus Raises Lazarus from the Dead

WHEN THE MESSENGER returned to the home of Martha, Mary, and Lazarus, he found Martha standing out front waiting for him.

"Where's Jesus?" she asked desperately.

"Coming later," the messenger replied warily, instinctively ducking his head from the torrent of reproving words he knew would come from the doughty head of household.

"What? Later?! What good is that going to do us? Lazarus could die tonight. Didn't you tell him what I told you to tell him? 'Lazarus, your friend, whom you love, is sick.' Those were my very words. I told you to tell him *that*. Did you?"

"Yes m'am, I did. He heard me, too. He looked at me close for a moment, then turned and said to his disciples, 'This will not end in death, but rather it is an occasion for the Son of God to be glorified. We're going to stay here for a couple more days.'"

"A couple more *days!*" gasped Martha. *Lazarus will be dead before he gets here,* she thought. She slunk back into the house to deliver the solemn news to Mary and Lazarus but had difficulty finding the right words. How could she tell her brother and sister that all hope was gone? How could she tell them he wasn't coming . . . in time.

In a matter of hours, Lazarus died. In keeping with local custom, his body was wrapped in spices and cloths and placed in a rocky tomb right away. The Judean climate was hot, and in a couple of days his mortal tissue would begin to decompose, to rot, to stink.

Perhaps Martha's reputation in the community began to sag as friends and neighbors muttered to one another, "I thought they were such close friends of the healer, Jesus of Nazareth. Surely he could have saved Lazarus if he had come on time. Apparently he had other business he considered more important. Maybe they're not such good friends as they claim."

The days went by slowly; until finally, four days after Lazarus had been placed in his stony grave, news came that Jesus was making his way toward Bethany and would be there soon. Martha could not contain herself but went charging out to meet him on the road into town. When she saw him, the first words that tumbled from her mouth were what she'd been thinking for a week.

"Lord, if you had been here, my brother would not have died!" She tried to hide her tone of reproach, the sadness, the hurt she felt. Then, softening, as ever she did in his actual presence, she breathed wistfully, "But even now, I know God will give you anything you ask of him." And Jesus responded directly to the deepest desire of her heart.

"Your brother will rise again."

Somewhat irked by this apparently pious platitude, the kind of thing insensitive people always say to those who have lost a loved one, Martha rebuffed him. "I know he will rise again in the great resurrection on the last day." *What, Jesus, don't you think I know my theology? I may be a woman, but I'm not ignorant. I know there's a great consolation coming some day, by and by, pie in the sky. Don't tell me that right now; I'm mourning the loss of my brother!*

But Jesus held her gaze and said, "I'm not talking eventualities and metaphysical eschatologies. I *am* the resurrection—and the life. If you believe that, you will never die. *Do* you believe, Martha?"

Suddenly she felt her heart burning as the truth bore through her, and she formed the necessary words: "Yes! I believe!"

She quickly sent for her sister, knowing something extraordinary was imminent. Mary came running from the house, and the crowd of mourners followed her, thinking she was headed for the tomb to wail.

Jesus asked that they show him where Lazarus was entombed. When they came to the desolate scene, in all its banal, dry, dusty reality, Jesus could not pretend to be unmoved. He broke down weeping along with all those broken souls who'd suffered inconsolable loss. The muttering voices in the background continued to voice disappointment in Jesus' late and apparently now useless appearance on the scene, but that did not deter *him*. He gathered his composure and commanded that the stone be rolled away from Lazarus's tomb. Martha tried to dissuade him, knowing that the horrible stench of death would come rolling out of that dark hole in the ground the moment the stone was lifted. But Jesus reminded her, "I told you that if you *believe*, you will see the glory of God."

He briefly addressed his Father in heaven aloud so that those around could hear his words, thanking him for hearing him and for answering his prayer. Then he raised his voice and called out, "Lazarus, come out of there!"

And he did! Still wrapped in his burial strips and bandages, the man Lazarus rose from death and returned to life. They quickly unwrapped the cloths and rejoiced. Lazarus lived among his family and neighbors for some time afterward, living proof of the glory and power of God.

Read more about this Lazarus-raising miracle in John 11:1–44.

Dead Man Walking

Jesus, the Son of God, Rises from the Dead

DEAD MAN WALKING. Dead man walking here!" This is the traditional cry of the prison guard as he leads a prisoner on death row to the place of execution. If you saw the 1995 film *Dead Man Walking*, you saw a scene such as this reenacted in a poignant way. The prisoner, Matthew Poncelet, found redemption, even though he was about to be executed for crimes he had committed.

Jesus was executed at the order of Pilate and also at the will of the Jewish leaders and the crowd that suddenly turned against him. Unlike Poncelet, Jesus had committed no crimes. Yet he suffered a horrible, grisly death on the cross.

The third day after Jesus' death began with a somber task that had to be performed. The Sabbath was now over. The women who followed Jesus—Mary Magdalene, Mary the mother of James (the disciple of Jesus), and others—wanted to anoint his body one last time as a memorial. Imagine that bitter walk to the tomb—the borrowed tomb in which Jesus lay. Hearing birds chirping would have been an insult, as was the thought that the sun could rise again on such a day.

Who would roll away the heavy stone sealed with Pilate's seal in front of the tomb? Would the guards who stood at the tomb to catch any would-be body snatchers move it? Those were the questions in their minds. But as they approached the tomb, the women found the issue of the stone a moot point.

The Gospel of Matthew details the earthquake that signaled the arrival of an angel who sent the stone rolling as if it were a pebble. Talk about an entrance!

How fitting that once again an earthquake signaled something important in relationship to Jesus. Just as Jesus died, an earthquake split the ground in two, as if the earth itself couldn't bear to witness the sight of the sinless Son of God dying for mankind (see Matthew 27:51). But now the earth shook once more as the angel—with a sonic boom rivaling any produced by a jet fighter—landed.

As with all of the appearances of God's messengers, everyone in the vicinity felt terrified. But this angel had good news—great news. Jesus was no longer in the tomb. He was alive!

The women ran off to tell the disciples. What a different conversation this must have been in comparison to the one on the way to the tomb.

Peter had denied Jesus three times (see Matthew 26:69–75) and was miserable in the aftermath. But when he heard from the women that Jesus was not in the tomb, he took off running with John just ahead of him. Peter, ever the impulsive one, entered the tomb first. No Jesus! Only the burial cloths that once bound his body occupied the tomb.

So it was true. Jesus was alive!

Perhaps the discouragement that coursed through Peter for days was rolled away, just as the stone had been. Perhaps he recalled Jesus' words to Martha just before her brother Lazarus rose from the dead: "I am the resurrection and the life. The one who believes in Me, even if he dies, will live" (John 11:25 HCSB).

But Mary Magdalene still had doubts as she paced the garden site of the tomb. Suppose someone took Jesus' body and hid it somewhere. How on earth would she ever find it? And why would someone take his body in the first place?

She gazed inside the tomb, as if looking in it could somehow solve the mystery of Jesus' whereabouts. Inside she found two angels in a tableau reminiscent of the angels on top of the ark of the covenant (see Exodus 25:19)—one angel at the head and one at the foot of the place where Jesus had lain.

Whether or not she recognized them as angels, the Bible does not say. After asking them the whereabouts of Jesus' body, her question was soon answered by a man who suddenly stood behind her.

Was he the gardener—the one in charge of the upkeep of the area? He would know where Jesus' body had been taken.

But instead of giving her a "Well, you see it's like this" explanation, all the man said was . . . her name. "Mary." Then she knew. The man was Jesus. He was alive!

The day that began with the sun rising just as it always did, even against the bitter wishes of those who grieved, now added another Son, also rising—the one they realized was more than just a man. He was God. And because of him, those who believe in him, though they die, will live once again too.

Read about the Resurrection in Matthew 28:1–13; Mark 16:1–8; Luke 24:1–12; and John 20:1–18.

Speaking in Tongues

The Holy Spirit's Arrival Causes the Disciples to Speak in Different Languages

DURING THE United Nations sessions, simultaneous translators work quickly to translate what the delegates say. A world with so many different spoken languages makes the need for translators imperative. But at the Pentecost feast in Jerusalem, no translators were needed even though many different languages were spoken. Everyone instantly understood what each of the disciples was saying. How could that be?

Before Jesus left earth, he reminded his disciples of the promise to send the Holy Spirit. "Do not leave Jerusalem, but wait for the gift my Father promised, which you have heard me speak about. For John baptized with water, but in a few days you will be baptized with the Holy Spirit" (Acts 1:4–5 NIV).

On Pentecost, fifty days after the Passover feast, the disciples were gathered in a house with many others. The sound of a powerful wind abruptly whistled through the house. Soon, small flames appeared above the heads of each person present. Only God could make an entrance like that. The Holy Spirit had come! Instantly, each person was filled with the presence of the Holy Spirit.

Everyone suddenly began to speak in other languages. Unlike at the tower of Babel (see Genesis 11) where a confusion of languages ended the camaraderie, speaking other languages here caused community, thanks to the Holy Spirit.

In Jerusalem, many people from other nations had gathered—a

gathering that might have seemed like an ancient form of the United Nations. These visitors suddenly heard the disciples and the others from the house speaking in the languages of the visitors' lands. But how could this be? The disciples were unschooled ex-fishermen from Galilee. How could they know the languages of the Medes, Asia, Egypt, Rome, and other such places?

With many crowds come hecklers. Someone in the crowd suddenly quipped that the disciples were drunk, which put a damper on the joy.

Peter had to get up and set the record straight. After assuring the crowd that no one would be drunk at nine in the morning, he quoted from the Old Testament prophet Joel to remind them of God's promise to send his Spirit: "I will pour out my Spirit in those days, . . . and your sons and daughters will prophesy" (Joel 2:28–29 NIV). He then went on to talk about Jesus—how he was crucified but had returned to life. Jesus, the Son of David, was greater than Israel's beloved king, David.

On that day, three thousand people believed in Jesus. This was the biggest catch of the former fisherman's life. Peter and his fellow disciples would continue to reel in others, thanks to the presence of the Holy Spirit.

To read more about the arrival of the Holy Spirit, read Acts 2:1–41.

The Man on the Mat

Peter Tells Aeneas to Stand on His Own Two Feet

WHEN PERSECUTION burst upon the early church in the city of Jerusalem, believers discreetly "emigrated" elsewhere. (In other words, they fled for their lives.) They went everywhere, and everywhere they went, they preached the gospel of Jesus Christ. New groups of believers began to dot the map throughout the Roman empire.

Peter, the apostle appointed to oversee the entire operation from the beginning, traveled about the country visiting the embryonic churches (see Acts 9:32). His ministry of consolidating and encouraging the new believers certainly corresponded to the charge Jesus had given him on the shores of the Sea of Galilee: "Peter, if you love me, tend my sheep. Take care of my sheep. Feed my sheep" (see John 21:15–19). For a burly fisherman used to the wind and waves on his face, traveling around to care for newly founded churches may have lacked the excitement of his previous career. But he did what his Master told him to do; he cared for the Master's sheep.

Pretty soon, he would have more excitement than he would know what to do with.

It happened in the little town of Lydda. He encountered a man named Aeneas who had been lying in bed, paralyzed, for eight years. *Now this is more like it,* he thought. Not hesitating a moment, Peter did what he knew well how to do. He barked out a hoarse command, "Aeneas, Jesus Christ heals you! Get up, and roll up your sleeping mat!" (Acts 9:34 NLT).

The man immediately got to his feet and stood up, eyeball-to-eyeball with Peter. Imagine it—the first time he'd been on his feet in over eight years! Then he picked up his mat, as he'd been told to do, and walked out.

Though Peter was not surprised by the power of Jesus' name to work miracles, the rest of the town was. When they saw what happened to Aeneas, folks in Lydda and in the neighboring city of Sharon all "turned to the Lord" (Acts 9:35).

Peter was tickled to be back in action and see God working miracles. He even accepted an invitation a few days later to come pay his respects at nearby Joppa, where a believer named Dorcas had just died . . . You can probably guess what he did there (see "She's Come Undone" below).

For more about Peter and the mat-toting man, read Acts 9:32–35.

She's Come Undone

When a Seamstress's Life Unravels, Peter Reconnects the Threads

MOST OF US like a story with a happy ending. We like to read about the poor but kind waitress who is given a lottery ticket worth millions, or the sick child in need of an emergency transplant who receives the organ just in the nick of time. But some stories don't end happily. A dedicated missionary who only wants to reach people with the gospel is killed. A friend dies of cancer. That's the reality of life here on earth. Tabitha's story didn't end happily either . . . at first.

We find her described in the book of Acts: "In Joppa there was a disciple named Tabitha (which, when translated, is Dorcas), who was always doing good and helping the poor" (Acts 9:36 NIV). There she was making clothes for the poor and doing other deeds that probably wouldn't be front-page news. But her life hit a snag and unraveled when she became seriously ill and died. Perhaps they began carving her epitaph: "Tabitha, also known as Dorcas, lived a quiet life of helpful service."

Some of the believers there asked Peter to come to Joppa. Why was Peter involved? At this point, many of the apostles were traveling about, establishing churches and spreading the gospel. They were being obedient to the commission Jesus gave them before he returned to heaven (see Matthew 28:18–20). So Peter was a travelin' man, helping to build up the often-persecuted church.

The disciples in the area near Joppa hoped Peter could do something or at least encourage the believers who were mourning. They took him to where Dorcas was laid, and the widows showed him all the wonderful clothes she had made for them. "See this? See?" they probably said. "She was a good woman."

Peter was around when Jesus raised Jairus's daughter from the dead (see "Girl, Get Up!" p. 221), and he knew miracles were possible. He also knew this was a time for prayer rather than despair. That could have been Jesus' motto. Peter sent everyone out of the room and got on his knees. After praying, he didn't hesitate as he told the dead woman, "Tabitha, get up" (Acts 9:40 NIV). And she did!

And with that, the threads of Dorcas's life were rewoven, thanks to the apostle Peter and the power of the Holy Spirit.

Some stories, it seems, do have happy endings.

Read the full story of how Dorcas returned to life in Acts 9:36–42.

The Centurion Seeks

The Gospel Goes to the Gentiles, after a Vision and a Little Nudge from God

W̲E̲ A̲L̲L̲ G̲E̲T̲ U̲S̲E̲D̲ to our comfort zones—that's why they're comfortable! Even in today's progressive society, some people still have difficulty crossing the imaginary barriers between cultures. Peter had the same problem almost two thousand years ago.

Cornelius and Peter couldn't have been more different.

Cornelius was Roman (a Gentile), wealthy, and a military man, whereas Peter was a Jew, got by with meager finances, and was a fisherman turned evangelist. What's more, a whole slew of laws kept Jews from eating certain foods and hanging out with Gentiles, for fear of being considered "unclean" (see Leviticus 11). But God was about to knock down the barriers.

Even though his people conquered Israel, Cornelius didn't cruelly oppress others. Instead, he prayed to the God of Israel and used his money to help the poor. Because he consistently sought the Lord, God sent an angel with a message for Cornelius: go to Joppa and look for a man named Simon.

Meanwhile in Joppa, Peter saw a vision. "He saw heaven opened and something like a large sheet being let down to earth by its four corners. It contained all kind of four-footed animals, as well as reptiles of the earth and birds of the air" (Acts 10:11–12 NIV). Then a voice spoke to Peter, telling him to get up, kill something, and eat it. For a man who had never broken a dietary law, this command had to be puzzling. After Peter's refusal to eat anything unclean, the voice replied, "Do not call anything impure that God has made clean" (Acts 10:15).

While Peter was trying to figure out what the vision meant, servants of Cornelius showed up at his door. Through the Holy Spirit, Peter knew that he was to accompany them. Off they went to the home of Cornelius—a home Peter would never have entered without the prompting of the Holy Spirit.

Upon Peter's arrival, the great and well-respected Roman bowed before Peter, a man the Romans usually oppressed. What a twist, especially since the house was filled with Cornelius's family and friends—all part of the ruling class of Romans.

Peter could have been arrogant, but instead he reminded Cornelius that they were both only men—men equal in the sight of God. It seems that Peter now understood the meaning of his vision.

Through miraculous angel visits and visions, God made it clear to both men—and everyone with them—that salvation was for everyone. Before his vision, Peter might have thought it impossible for a Roman to convert to Christianity. But now he understood that he was to share the gospel with every person with whom he came into contact, regardless of race, culture, language, or economic standing.

When Peter began to share the gospel, God confirmed his approval by filling all those present with the Holy Spirit. God rewarded the faithful seeker, Cornelius, with a treasure beyond anything he could have imagined—a place in the family of God.

To read all about Cornelius and Peter, go to Acts 10.

Snake Surprise

Paul Gets the Surprise of His Life When a Poisonous Snake Bites Him

IF YOU'VE EVER been camping in a remote place, you're aware of the possibility of finding a snake coiled up somewhere you least hope to find one. Many snakes are harmless. But some snakes, like the viper, have a poisonous bite. The apostle Paul learned that firsthand (pun intended, as you'll see in a minute).

The apostle Paul had been having one of those weeks where everything seemed to go wrong. (Actually, he had the kind of *life* where everything seemed to go wrong. You know—beatings, being nearly stoned to death, jail sentences, court trials. But that was the price he paid for being a follower of Jesus.) He was on his way to Rome to continue standing trial for the simple fact that he believed Jesus was everything he claimed to be. As a Roman citizen, he had the right to appeal to Caesar. But on his way to Rome, a terrible storm occurred at sea, forcing aground the ship he was on. Now the real possibility of being shipwrecked on an island was before him and the rest of the people aboard the ship.

After dragging his tired body out of the water, the ever-practical Paul set about building a fire—always a good idea when one has barely survived drowning and wants to escape hypothermia. And that's when it happened—the snake surprise.

A viper suddenly appeared and clamped down on Paul's hand! Perhaps the viper had been hiding in the wood Paul gathered and was surprised by the sudden spurt of flame. In any case, it bit down and would not let go. The perfect ending for an awful day.

Some viper bites are fatal and some aren't, depending upon the type of viper. All viper bites are painful, however. The type that bit Paul had to be the fatal venom kind. After all, the people on the island assumed that Paul had to be deserving of being bitten by a poisonous snake. Their instant assessment branded him a murderer who would finally receive his just deserts. He might have cheated death by escaping the storm at sea, but he would soon die from the snakebite. Mark their words.

To their surprise, Paul didn't die. But the snake probably did, once Paul shook it into the flames it had tried to avoid. To add insult to injury, in the minds of the islanders, Paul didn't even get sick!

Whoa. What kind of man was he? One who deserved their worship, in their opinion. But Paul knew that he was just a man—just a man protected by the real God.

Paul's snaky peril is recorded in Acts 28:1–6.

Index

Printed in the United States
By Bookmasters